European Architecture in Details

The Deutsche Nationalbibliothek lists this publication in the Deutsche Nationalbibliografie; detailed bibliographical data are available on the internet at http://dnb.d-nb.de.

ISBN 978-3-03768-086-5

© 2012 by Braun Publishing AG
www.braun-publishing.ch

1st edition 2012

Editor: Markus Sebastian Braun
Editorial staff: Anne Osherson, Manuela Roth
Text Cities: Markus Hattstein
Translation preface: Dagmar Glück (German version), Marcel Saché (French version)
Graphic concept and layout: Manuela Roth, Berlin

All of the information in this volume has been compiled to the best of the editor's knowledge. It is based on the information provided to the publisher. The publisher assumes no responsibility for its accuracy or completeness as well as copyright discrepancies and refers to the specified sources. All rights to the photographs are property of the photographer (please refer to the picture credits).

Picture Credits:

Amsterdam, Berlin: Marius Flucht – www.herrflucht.de
Athína, Budapest, Praha: Johannes Kramer
Barcelona, Wien: Thomas Kierok – www.kierok.de
Bruxelles, Berlin: Kai Senf – www.kaisenf.com
Helsinki: Dominik Butzmann – www.dbutzmann.de
Istanbul, Roma: Bernhardt Link – www.link-foto.de
Kraków: Katja Zimmermann – www.frauzimmermann.com
Lisboa, Berlin, Riga, Stockholm: Claudia Weidemann
Ljubljana, London, Vilnius: Katja Hoffmann – www.katjahoffmann.de
Paris: Marion Lammersen – www.marionlammersen.com
Sankt-Peterburg: Claudia Bull – www.bulldesign.de
Zürich: Markus Sebastian Braun, Thomas Kierok

European
Architecture
in
Details

BRAUN

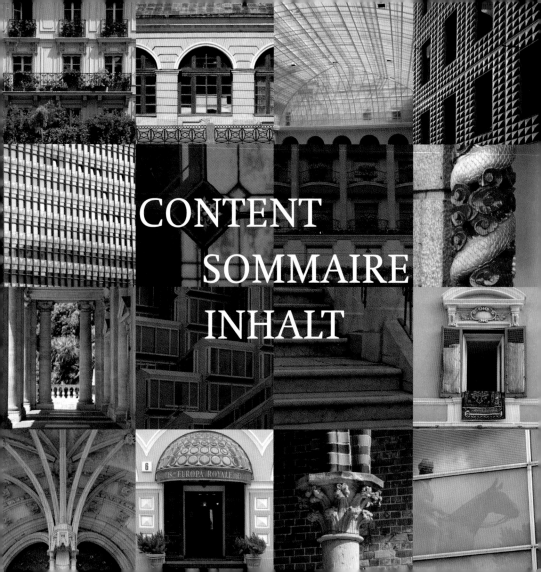

CONTENT
SOMMAIRE
INHALT

PREFACE

When most people speak about European architecture, whether they focus on the majestic castles and monuments of the past or on the sleek, hyper-modern buildings of the present, they speak in broad terms and generalizations. Paris is characterized by its wide boulevards, Athens is defined by the extensive marble legacies of past empires, and few can avoid mentioning "Soviet-style buildings" when describing their impressions of St. Petersburg and the rest of the former Eastern bloc. Only the biggest buildings and the most recognizable landmarks ever seem worthy of mention, as if only the most familiar sights embody the very essence of an intricate metropolis. Whether this fascination with the large-scale is a symptom of our increasingly fast-paced lives, or simply human nature, this approach to architecture will never deliver the full picture.

European Architecture in Details aims to take a deeper look, inviting you on a colorful tour through the squares, boulevards, and alleys of 21 of Europe's most splendid cities. Instead of standing back and admiring dizzying new heights, or the ensemble effect of a street full of historical buildings, it shines a spotlight on the details. The doors, the stairs, the windows and balconies – all these elements must come together in any impressive feat of architecture, but are rarely appreciated as stand-alone accomplishments. Now, they finally come into their own, as the protagonists. Can you recognize London by its pillars? Do the windows of Helsinki and Stockholm accommodate a particularly Northern point of view? How do façades on the Baltic coast compare to those found along the Alps? Whether or not you find yourself able to answer these questions, you are sure to see each of these cities in a whole new light after discovering the many unique facets of architecture that are so rarely noticed. Instead of only focusing on a few of the biggest sights of each city, looking at all the details together reveals a beautiful and complex mosaic. From classical Southern European ports like Lisbon to stylish and lively Scandinavian metro areas and the revitalized capitals of Eastern Europe like Riga and Vilnius, each city has its own unique character, as well as its own story. Throughout this journey, cutting-edge contemporary design and ancient architectural legacies are seamlessly woven together to create their different identities, reflecting the cities' individual pasts, as well as one feature that they all share: constant evolution.

This book provides snapshots of the different facets of early 21st century Europe, with the understanding that no city, no matter how beautiful, can remain frozen in time. Of course, some of the architecture presented here has already existed for centuries, like the numerous churches and synagogues that have stood fast through Europe's most tumultuous years, or even millennia, in the case of the magnificent remains of the Colosseum in Rome, and many buildings will continue to be preserved well into the future. Others, however, will have to make room for the new. The details that they contribute to their city will either endure, or vanish along with them, only to be replaced by new architecture, with new intricacies, continuing the cycle of renovation and transformation that has been in motion since the very beginning of construction.

Dozens of high-quality photographs have been collected for each of the 21 European cities featured here, in order to provide a comprehensive view of their details and hidden qualities. This may include a closer look at certain specific features of already well-known buildings, like the corniches of Barcelona's legendary Sagrada Família or grandiose columns of Istanbul's Topkapi palace, or there may be details that simply stand out in ordinary streets or forgotten façades. Each city is accompanied by a short introduction, but as always, the images speak for themselves.

Markus Sebastian Braun

PRÉFACE

Qu'il s'agisse des majestueux châteaux et monuments d'autrefois ou des élégantes réalisations contemporaines, l'architecture européenne est habituellement présentée de manière globale et indifférenciée : on évoque les larges boulevards de Paris, les grands ensembles en marbre construits jadis à Athènes ou les bâtiments « de style soviétique » qui caractérisent Saint-Pétersbourg et d'autres villes de l'ancien bloc de l'Est, comme si seuls les édifices les plus imposants et les plus remarquables étaient dignes d'attention ou susceptibles d'incarner l'essence même d'une ville, ensemble forcément complexe. Que cette fascination pour la grandeur soit le reflet de notre mode de vie toujours plus rapide ou qu'elle corresponde simplement à la nature humaine, elle ne saurait rendre compte de l'architecture européenne de manière exhaustive.

L'ouvrage *European Architecture in Details* offre une toute autre approche des rues et places de vingt-et-une des plus belles villes d'Europe : plutôt que de prendre du recul pour admirer en bloc des alignements de bâtiments historiques ou des immeubles modernes toujours plus hauts, ce livre se focalise sur les détails architecturaux tels que portes,

fenêtres, balcons et escaliers, rarement appréciés à leur juste valeur. Ces réalisations, qui contribuent largement au charme de toute architecture, sont ainsi les véritables protagonistes de l'ouvrage.

Est-il possible de reconnaître Londres à ses colonnes ? Les fenêtres de Stockholm ou Helsinki rendent-elles compte d'un style typique de l'Europe du Nord ? Qu'est-ce qui distingue les façades baltiques de celles des pays alpins ? Que vous soyez ou non capable de répondre d'emblée à ces questions, l'ouvrage *European Architecture in Details* vous permettra de découvrir des aspects de toutes ces villes passant souvent inaperçus en dépit de leur grand intérêt architectural. Ce livre, qui ne se concentre pas sur quelques bâtiments seulement, s'attache à une multitude de détails de manière à créer une mosaïque d'une beauté et d'une complexité impressionnantes.

Lisbonne et les autres villes baroques des pays du sud de l'Europe, de même que Riga, Vilnius et les capitales revitalisées d'Europe de l'Est, ont chacune un caractère qui leur est propre et s'enracine dans leur histoire. Le livre met en évidence les liens qui unissent le patrimoine bâti et l'architecture contemporaine, c'est-à-dire l'évolution constante de ces organismes vivants et personnalisés que sont les villes européennes. Il met également l'accent sur les différentes facettes de l'architecture du début du XXIe siècle de manière à souligner qu'aucune ville, aussi belle soit elle, ne saurait se figer sur son passé.

On y trouvera également des édifices ayant défié les siècles voire les millénaires — notamment des églises, des synagogues ou le Colisée de Rome —, certains devant être conservés tandis que d'autres cèderont un jour la place à de nouvelles réalisations. Les détails architecturaux qu'ils intègrent, typiques de leur lieu d'implantation, seront eux aussi conservés ou détruits, s'inscrivant ainsi dans le mouvement incessant de rénovation et transformation qui, depuis toujours, caractérise l'activité des bâtisseurs.

Un grand nombre de photos de haute qualité prises dans les vingt-et-une ville d'Europe sélectionnées offrent un panorama complet des détails architecturaux. Certains clichés sont comme un coup de projecteur sur des bâtiments apparemment anodins, tandis que d'autres illustrent des détails d'édifices célèbres comme la Sagrada Familia de Barcelone

ou le palais de Topkapi à Istanbul. Chaque ville est présentée par un texte court mais comme d'habitude, les photos sont particulièrement éloquentes.

Markus Sebastian Braun

VORWORT

Ist von europäischer Architektur die Rede, dann meist in allgemein gehaltenen Begriffen und Generalisierungen, unabhängig davon ob sich das Gespräch um majestätische Schlösser, um Monumente vergangener Jahrhunderte oder die hyper-modernen Bauwerke der Gegenwart dreht. Paris, das sind die breiten Boulevards. Athen ist auf Marmor gebaut, dem Erbe der alten Griechen. Geht es um den ehemaligen Ostblock, kommen die wenigsten umhin, die Gebäude „Sowjetischen Stils" zu beschreiben, beispielsweise, wenn sie ihre Eindrücke von St. Petersburg schildern. Es scheint, als seien nur die auffälligsten Bauwerke und Wahrzeichen einer Erwähnung wert, als verkörperten sie allein das Wesen einer ganzen Metropole. Die Faszination für das Große und Imposante mag ein Symptom unserer immer schneller werdenden Zeit sein oder es entspricht einfach der menschlichen Natur. Diese Herangehensweise an Architektur kann jedoch niemals ein vollständiges Bild ergeben.

European Architecture in Details will genauer hinschauen und lädt zu einem Streifzug durch die 21 spannendsten Städte Europas ein, über ihre farbenfrohe Plätze, durch Boulevards und Alleen. Während der Betrachter gewöhnlich einen Schritt zurück tritt, um in schwindelerregende Höhen zu blicken oder den Ensemble-Effekt einer Straße mit historischen Gebäuden zu bewundern, geht *European Architecture in Details* ganz nah heran und eröffnet so eine völlig neue Perspektive. Sind es doch Feinheiten wie Türen, Treppen, Fenster und Balkone, die eine architektonische Leistung erst ausmachen. Gerade diese Meisterleistungen im Kleinen werden nur selten in ihrer Eigenständigkeit wahrgenommen und kaum angemessen gewürdigt. Endlich sind sie die Protagonisten. Ist es möglich anhand einzelner Säulen London zu erkennen? Vermögen Fenster in Helsinki und Stockholm die skandinavische Architektur zu repräsentieren? Ähneln Fassaden im Baltikum jenen entlang der Alpen? Egal ob sich diese Fragen beantworten lassen, wird eines deutlich: Sobald man ins Detail geht, erscheint jede Stadt durch ihre einzigartigen architektonischen Facetten in ganz neuem Licht. Wenn man einmal davon absieht, nur die bekanntesten Sehenswürdigkeiten einer Stadt zu betrachten, wird man erkennen, wie aus all den kleinen Details ein wunderschönes, komplexes Mosaik entsteht.

Von den klassischen südeuropäischen Hafenstädten wie Lissabon über die dynamischen

Metropolen Skandinaviens bis hin zu den wiederbelebten Hauptstädten Osteuropas wie Riga und Vilnius, besitzt jede Stadt einen einzigartigen Charakter und ihre eigene Geschichte. Auf der Reise in den Mikrokosmos der Städte verschmilzt modernes zeitgenössisches Design mit dem architektonischen Erbe der Antike. Die Details schaffen dabei Identität und spiegeln die individuelle Vergangenheit der Städte wider. Dabei wird allerdings auch eine Gemeinsamkeit sichtbar: Die europäischen Metropolen sind ständig in Bewegung.

Der vorliegende Band ist eine Momentaufnahme der unterschiedlichen Facetten Europas im frühen 21. Jahrhundert und zeigt, dass die Zeit selbst in den schönsten Städten niemals stillsteht. Ein Teil der präsentierten Architektur existiert seit langer Zeit, wie die zahlreichen Kirchen und Synagogen, die Europas turbulente Jahrhunderte überdauert haben, oder sogar seit Jahrtausenden, wie im Fall des prächtigen Kolosseums in Rom. Viele dieser Bauwerke werden auch in Zukunft Bestand haben. Andere müssen weichen, um Raum für Neues zu schaffen. Die Details, um die sie ihre Stadt bereichern, bleiben oder verschwinden mit den Gebäuden. Neue Architek-

turen mit neuen Feinheiten werden an ihre Stelle treten. So setzt sich der Kreislauf aus Erneuerung und Transformation fort, der die Baukunst seit ihrem Anbeginn auszeichnet.

Zahlreiche hochwertige Fotografien wurden zu jeder der 21 präsentierten Städte ausgewählt, um einen umfassenden Blick auf ihre jeweiligen Details und versteckten Qualitäten zu bieten. Dabei werden auch einige bekannte Bauwerke aus nächster Nähe betrachtet. Die zerklüftete Fassade der legendären Sagrada Família in Barcelona oder die beeindruckenden Säulen des Topkapi Palasts in Istanbul reihen sich nahtlos ein zwischen vergessene Fassaden und raffinierte Details, die aus gewöhnlichen Straßenzügen hervorstechen. Jedem der urbanen Mosaike ist eine kurze Einleitung vorangestellt, auch wenn die Bilder selbstverständlich für sich sprechen.

Markus Sebastian Braun

AMSTERDAM

Amsterdam may be known as the city of bicycles and canals, but its 1,300 bridges, thousands of shops and warehouses, as well as the Munt Tower and the old stock market recall its history as a wealthy trading and shipping center. Today, Amsterdam is also famous for its liberal, hedonistic scene.

La ville des vélos et des canaux est aussi connue pour ses 1 300 ponts, ses milliers de magasins et d'entrepôts, la tour de Munt et l'ancienne bourse, qui rappellent qu'Amsterdam était un grand centre de commerce maritime. Aujourd'hui, Amsterdam est aussi célèbre pour son style de vie hédoniste et permissif.

Als Stadt der Radfahrer und Grachten kündet Amsterdam mit seinen fast 1300 Brücken und Tausenden von Kaufmanns- und Lagerhäusern sowie dem Münzturm und der Alten Börse vom einstigen Wohlstand der See- und Fernhändler. Heute ist Amsterdam auch für den liberalen, lebenskünstlerischen Stil seiner Bewohner bekannt.

15

16

17

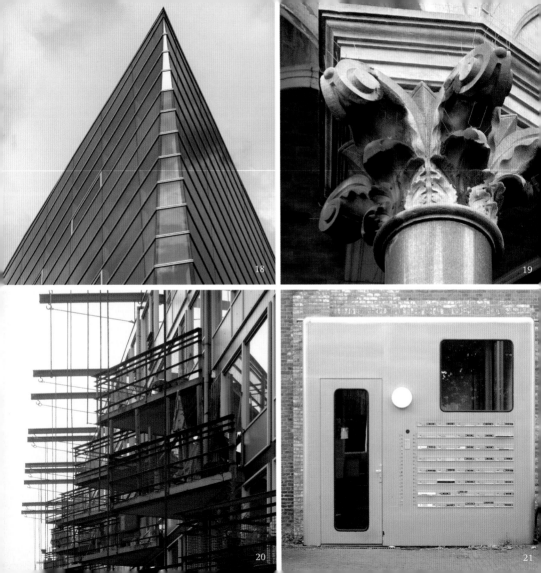

26

27

28

29

30

31

32

33

34

43

44

45

46

47

48

49

BOSS

50

51

52

53

(...) En dan begon 't te schemeren ,
één ging er vreeselijk te keer , vlak b
voet lag bijna in de sloot. And 54
heel ver weg. Een koe, die je nieuwe
halve duisternis, hoorde je lan
er een kl

55

56

57

62

63

64

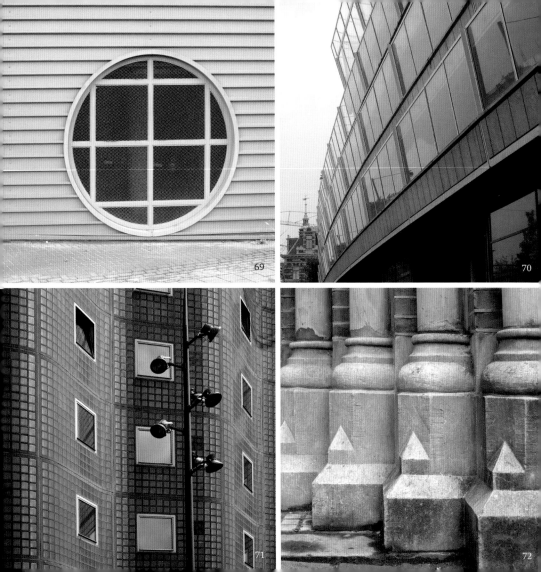

69

70

71

72

73

74

75

76

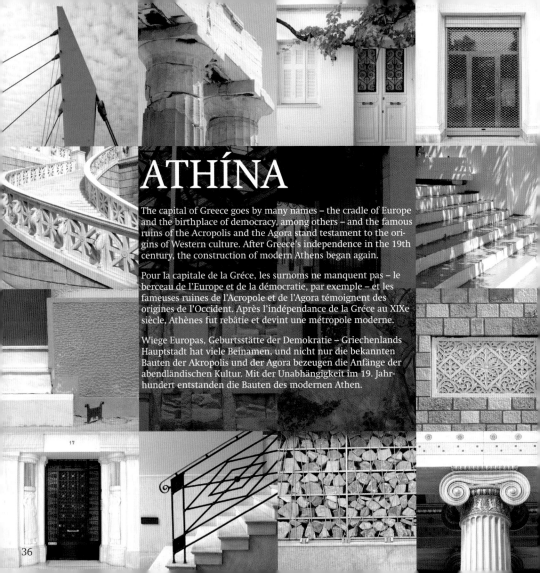

ATHÍNA

The capital of Greece goes by many names – the cradle of Europe and the birthplace of democracy, among others – and the famous ruins of the Acropolis and the Agora stand testament to the origins of Western culture. After Greece's independence in the 19th century, the construction of modern Athens began again.

Pour la capitale de la Gréce, les surnoms ne manquent pas – le berceau de l'Europe et de la démocratie, par exemple – et les fameuses ruines de l'Acropole et de l'Agora témoignent des origines de l'Occident. Après l'indépendance de la Gréce au XIXe siècle, Athènes fut rebâtie et devint une métropole moderne.

Wiege Europas, Geburtsstätte der Demokratie – Griechenlands Hauptstadt hat viele Beinamen, und nicht nur die bekannten Bauten der Akropolis und der Agora bezeugen die Anfänge der abendländischen Kultur. Mit der Unabhängigkeit im 19. Jahrhundert entstanden die Bauten des modernen Athen.

6

7

5

12

13

14

15

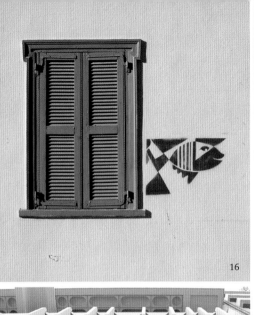

16

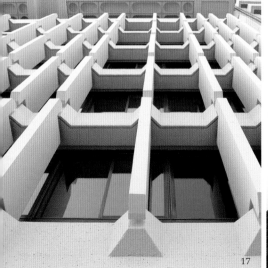

17

18

19

20

21

26

27

28

33

34

35

36

37

38

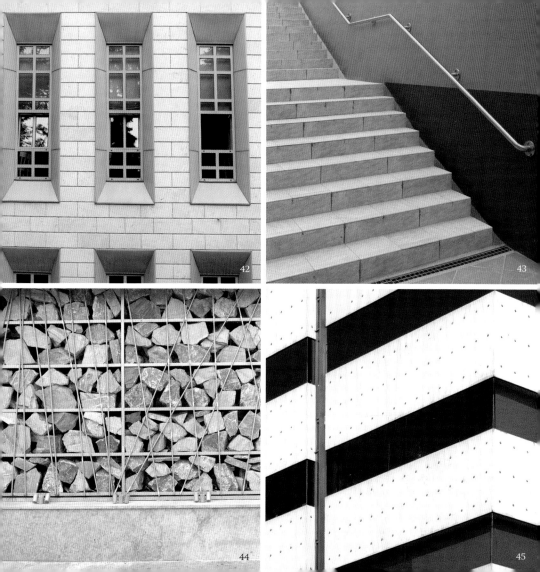

46

47

48

49

50

51

52

53

54

55

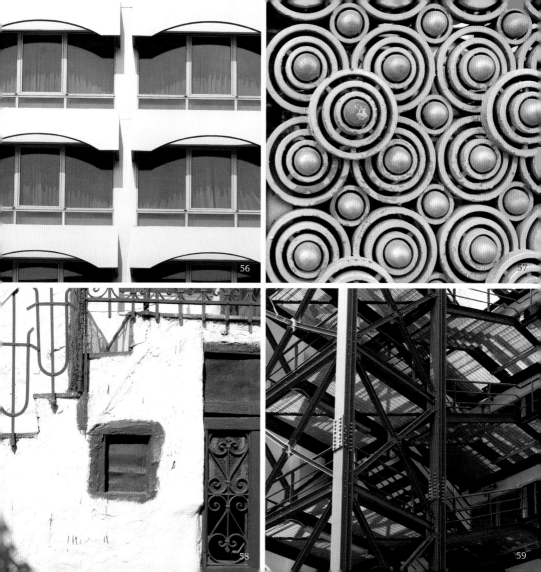

61

62

60

63

64

65

70

71

72

73

74

75

76

77

78

79

80

81

82

83

84

85

86

87

8

BARCELONA

The proudly independent capital of Catalonia developed its own Art Nouveau style during the Modernist period, and Antoni Gaudi's Sagrada Familia Cathedral, the crowning jewel of this movement, is still under construction today. The Gothic quarter, with its markets and arcades, stands out from the rest of the historical city center.

Fière et indépendante, la capitale de la Catalogne développa une grande tradition d'Art Nouveau pendant le mouvement Moderniste, dont la Sagrada Familia, la fameuse cathédrale inachevée d'Antoni Gaudi, est un des exemples les plus connus. Le quartier Gothique, avec ses marchés et ses arcades, se détache clairement du reste du centre historique de la ville.

Die Hauptstadt Kataloniens ist stets auf Eigenständigkeit bedacht und entwickelte mit dem „Modernisme" einen eigenen Jugendstil; dessen Symbol ist Antoni Gaudis Kathedrale Sagrada Familia, an der bis heute gebaut wird. Im historischen Stadtkern sticht besonders das Gotische Viertel mit seinen Märkten und Arkaden hervor.

7

9

10

11

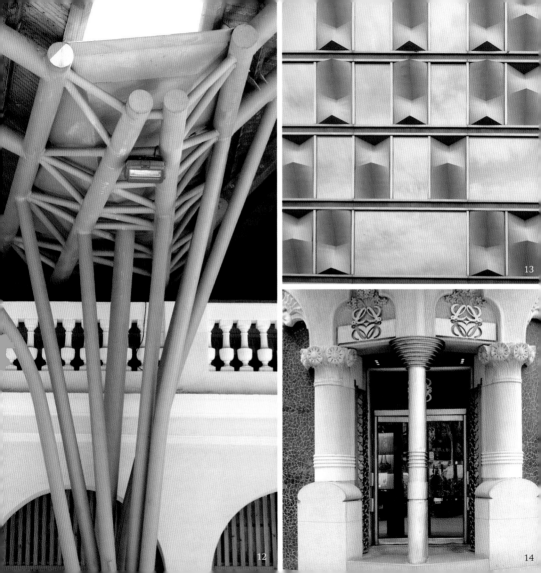

12

13

14

15

16

17

25

26

27

28

29

ES LLOGA
676714191

30

31

32

33

34

35

36

37

38

39

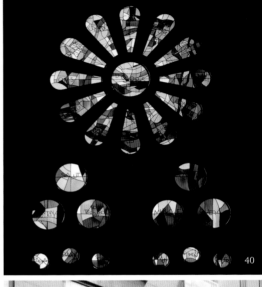

40

41

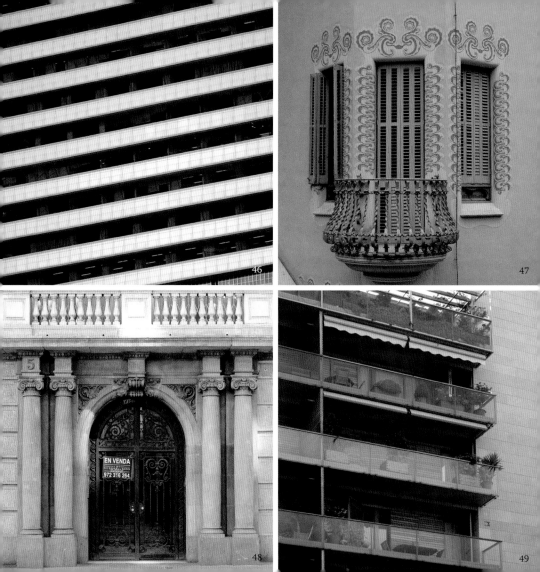

46

47

48

49

50

51

52

53

54

55

56

57

58

59

60

65

66

67

68

69

70

71

72

73

74

75

76

77

78

79

80

81

82

BERLIN

Gigantic construction projects and ambitious building plans leave Berlin in constant evolution, as the so-called "Athens of the Spree" of the Prussian empire absorbs modern spaces like Potsdamer Platz. The somewhat gruff warmth of Berliners suits this vibrant city.

Entre ses gigantesques projets de construction et ses plans de plus en plus ambitieux, Berlin reste en évolution constante. « L'Athènes sur la Spree » absorbe ainsi des espaces modernes comme Potsdamer Platz. La cordialité un peu bourrue des Berlinois convient bien à cette ville dynamique.

Gigantische Bauvorhaben und ehrgeizige Gestaltungspläne lassen Berlin niemals zur Ruhe kommen und verquicken das Spree-Athen der Preußenkönige mit modernsten Arealen wie dem Potsdamer Platz. Die etwas ruppige Herzlichkeit der Berliner – „Schnauze mit Herz" – passt zu dieser pulsierenden Stadt.

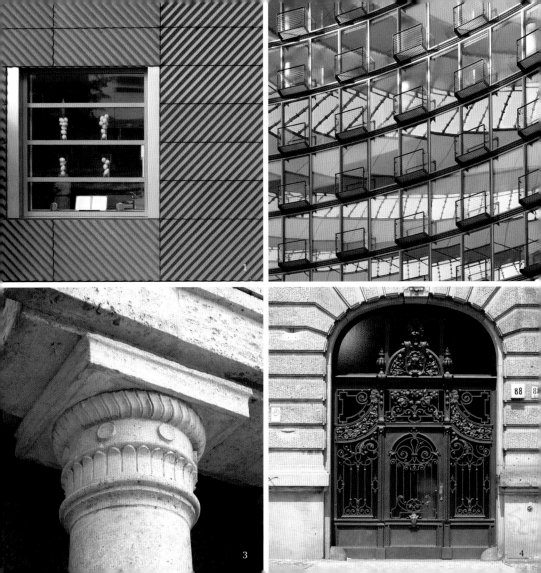

5

6

7

16

17

18

19

20

Eingang Süd

21

23

24

25

26

27

28

29

30

31

32

33

34

35

36

37

38

39

44

45

46

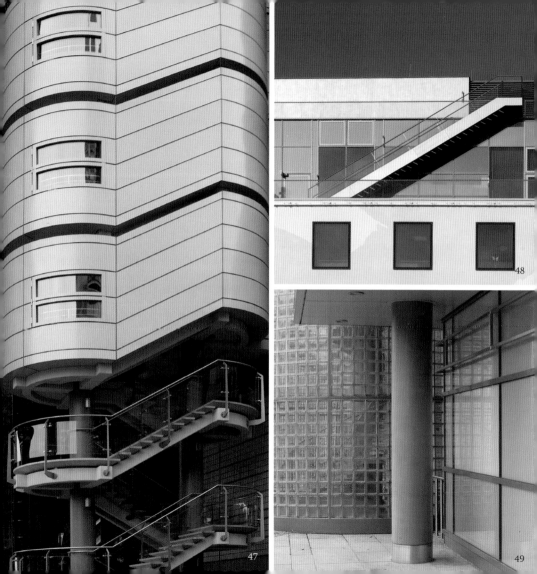

47

48

49

54

56

57

58

59

60

61

62

63

72

73

74

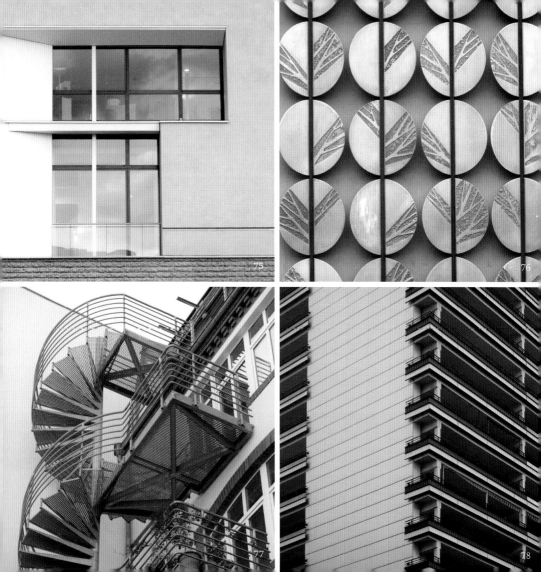

BRUXELLES

As the seat of NATO and of the EU, the "Capital of Europe" has international flair and features a mix of ultra-modern and traditional Flemish architecture. Brussels is the home of famous comic book characters, exquisite cuisine, wonderful beer and fine pralines.

En tant que siège de l'Union européenne et de l'OTAN, « la capitale de l'Europe » a un charme international ainsi qu'un mélange d'architecture ultra moderne et de traditions flamandes. Bruxelles est la ville des bandes dessinées, aussi bien qu'une capitale gastronomique, renommée pour sa bière et ses pralines.

Als Sitz der EU und der NATO hat die „Hauptstadt Europas" internationales Flair und besitzt einen spannenden Mix aus traditionell flandrischer und modernster Stadtarchitektur. Brüssel ist die Heimat bekannter Comicfiguren, einer exquisiten Küche, erlesener Biere und feinster Pralinen.

9

10

11

16

17

18

19

20

21

29
30
31

33

34

35

36

37

38

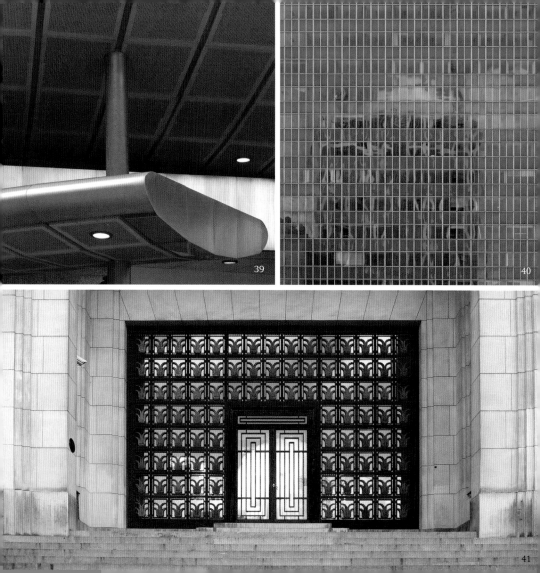

The Lobster Shop

Parking

42

43

44

45

LEONIDAS

50

51

52

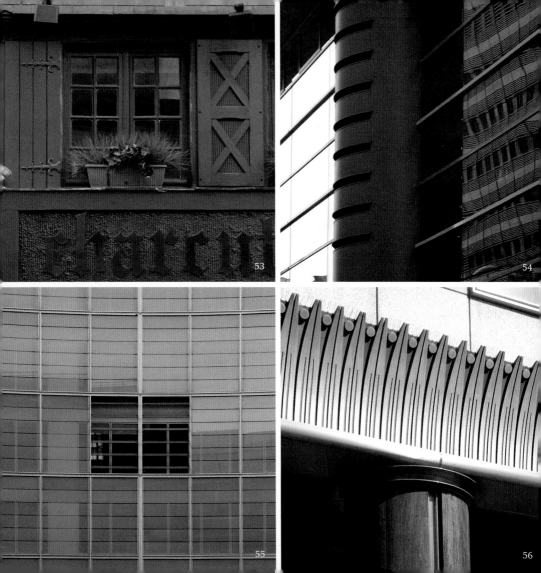

58

59

60

61

62

63

64

65

66

67

68

Danish Tavern

19

69

70

BUDAPEST

The twin cities of Buda and Pest, which were only recently joined with tremendous bridges, lie on both sides of the Danube river with their impressive buildings and streets. Echoes of the Magyars' long fight for independence can be felt throughout much of Budapest, which still functions as the mediator between Western and Eastern Europe.

Créée par la fusion des anciennes villes de Buda et de Pest, la capitale de l'Hongrie est située sur les deux rives du Danube, reliée par des immenses ponts et dotée de grandes rues et d'impressionnants bâtiments. La longue guerre d'indépendance des Magyars a laissé ses traces dans toute la ville, qui sert toujours de médiateur entre l'Est et l'Ouest.

Die erst spät zusammengewachsene Doppelstadt liegt – durch gewaltige Brücken verbunden – mit ihren beeindruckenden Bauten und Straßen zu beiden Seiten der Donau. Vieles in Budapest erzählt vom langen Freiheitskampf der Magyaren, die sich bis heute als Mittler zwischen West- und Osteuropa verstehen.

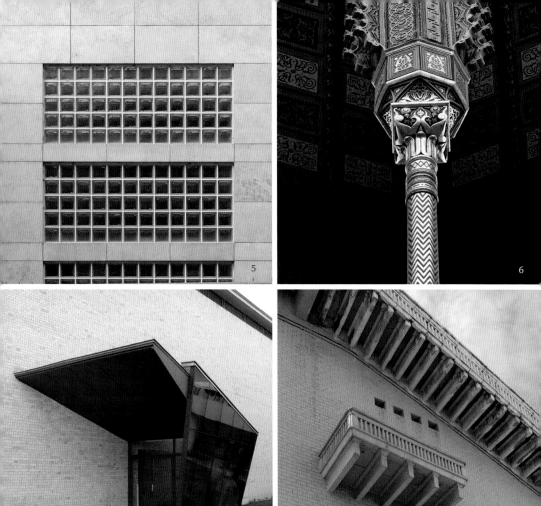

24

25

26

27

28

29

30

31

32

33

34

35

36

37

38

39

40

41

42

47

48

49

50

51

52

53

61

62

63

64

65

66

67

72

73

74

75

76

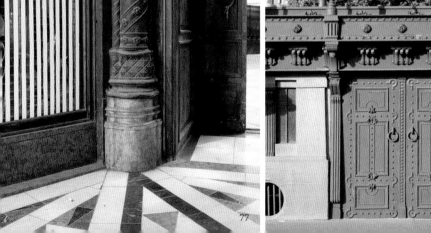

77

78

83

84

85

86

87

88

89

90

91

92

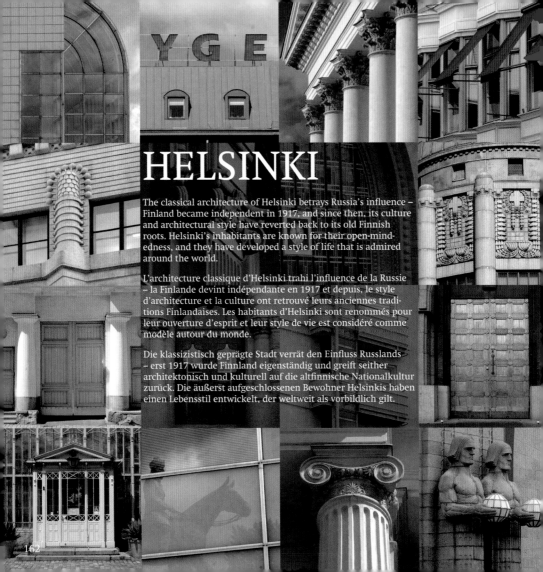

HELSINKI

The classical architecture of Helsinki betrays Russia's influence – Finland became independent in 1917, and since then, its culture and architectural style have reverted back to its old Finnish roots. Helsinki's inhabitants are known for their open-mindedness, and they have developed a style of life that is admired around the world.

L'architecture classique d'Helsinki trahi l'influence de la Russie – la Finlande devint indépendante en 1917 et depuis, le style d'architecture et la culture ont retrouvé leurs anciennes traditions Finlandaises. Les habitants d'Helsinki sont renommés pour leur ouverture d'esprit et leur style de vie est considéré comme modèle autour du monde.

Die klassizistisch geprägte Stadt verrät den Einfluss Russlands – erst 1917 wurde Finnland eigenständig und greift seither architektonisch und kulturell auf die altfinnische Nationalkultur zurück. Die äußerst aufgeschlossenen Bewohner Helsinkis haben einen Lebensstil entwickelt, der weltweit als vorbildlich gilt.

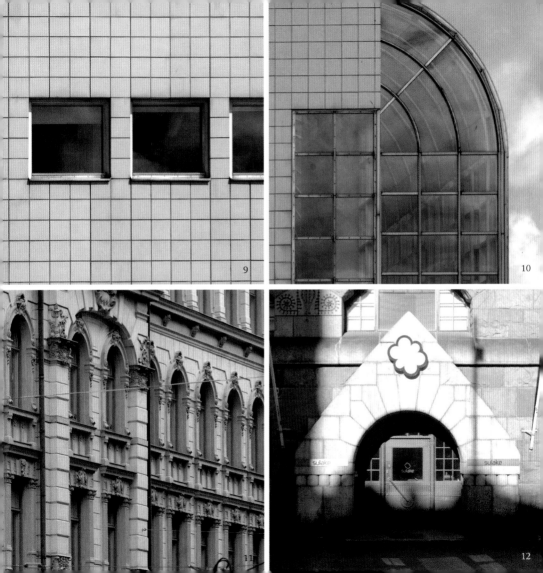

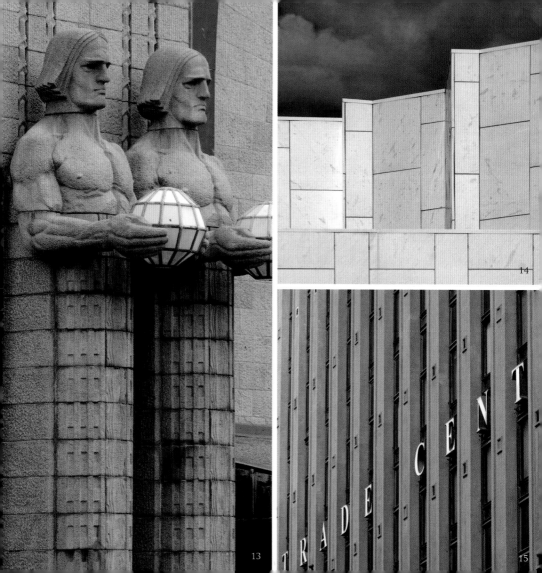

13

14

TRADE CENT

15

24

25

26

35

36

37

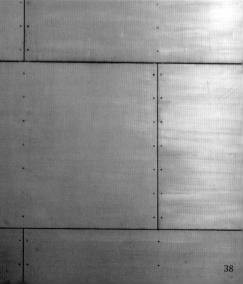

38

40

41

42

47

48

49

50

51

52

53

58

59

60

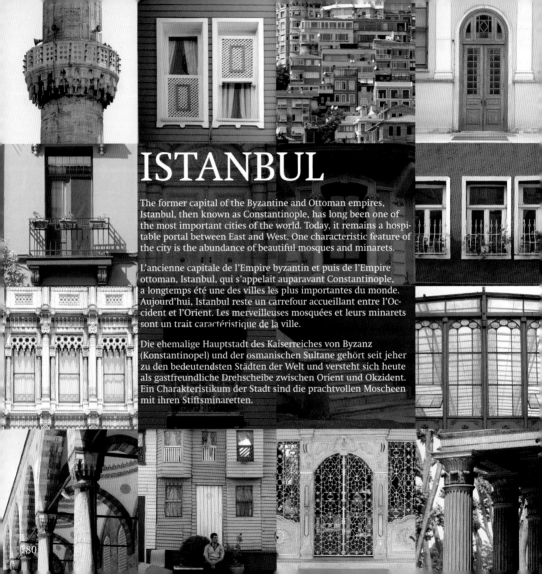

ISTANBUL

The former capital of the Byzantine and Ottoman empires, Istanbul, then known as Constantinople, has long been one of the most important cities of the world. Today, it remains a hospitable portal between East and West. One characteristic feature of the city is the abundance of beautiful mosques and minarets.

L'ancienne capitale de l'Empire byzantin et puis de l'Empire ottoman, Istanbul, qui s'appelait auparavant Constantinople, a longtemps été une des villes les plus importantes du monde. Aujourd'hui, Istanbul reste un carrefour accueillant entre l'Occident et l'Orient. Les merveilleuses mosquées et leurs minarets sont un trait caractéristique de la ville.

Die ehemalige Hauptstadt des Kaiserreiches von Byzanz (Konstantinopel) und der osmanischen Sultane gehört seit jeher zu den bedeutendsten Städten der Welt und versteht sich heute als gastfreundliche Drehscheibe zwischen Orient und Okzident. Ein Charakteristikum der Stadt sind die prachtvollen Moscheen mit ihren Stiftsminaretten.

17

18   19

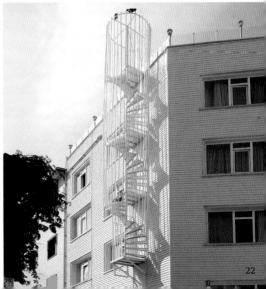

34

35

ZİNCİR 88

36

37

38

39

40

45

46

47

48

49

50

59

60

61

62

63

64

KRAKÓW

The old city of Krakow, home of the Wawel castle and the "King's Way", has long been the heart of Polish culture and national identity. The second oldest university city in Europe also boasts one of the most beautiful old towns, and is still a center for both science and Polish catholicism.

La vieille ville de Cracovie, où se trouve le château Wawel et « le chemin du roi » a longtemps été le centre de la culture et de l'identité nationale de la Pologne. La deuxième plus ancienne ville universitaire européenne est aussi dotée d'un des plus beaux centres historiques et reste un centre scientifique et religieux.

In der alten, stolzen Königsstadt mit der Burganlage Wawel und dem „Königsweg" schlug stets das Herz des polnischen Nationalbewusstseins. Die zweitälteste Universitätsstadt Europas besitzt eine der schönsten Altstädte und ist bis heute ein Zentrum der Wissenschaft und des polnischen Katholizismus.

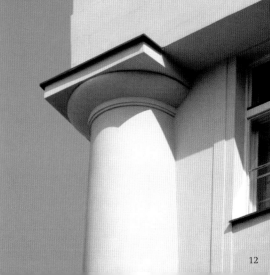

13

12

15

16

17

18

19

24

25

26

27

28

29

30

31

32

33

34

35

36

37

38

39

40

41

46

47

48

49

50

51

52

53

54

55

56

Jesper Alv~ & Isabel~osseová

58

59

60

61

62

67

68

69

LISBOA

The earthquake in 1755 meant that the old Baixa area had to be completely re-built, while the the upper Bairro Alto district was laid out above. The wide boulevards were modelled after Paris, and there are lookout points (miradouros) all over the city, with views of the Atlantic coast and the Tejo river.

Après le tremblement de terre en 1755, le vieux quartier de Baixa fut complètement reconstruit, tandis que le Bairro Alto s'étala au dessus. Les larges boulevards rappellent le style Parisien et des points de vue (miradouros) qui donnent sur la côte Atlantique et sur le Tejo sont répandus tout autour de la ville.

Das Erdbeben von 1755 ermöglichte eine völlige Neugestaltung der Altstadt Baixa, während oberhalb die Oberstadt Bairro Alto angelegt wurde. Die Prachtstraßen sind nach Pariser Vorbild gestaltet. Überall finden sich Aussichtspunkte (Miradouros) auf die Atlantikküste und den Fluss Tejo.

2

4

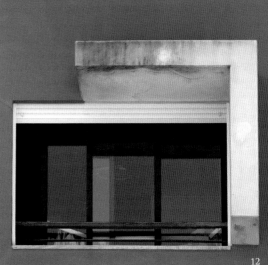

9

10

11

12

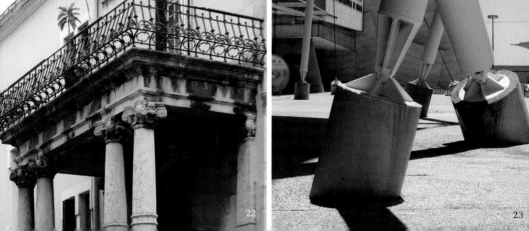

24

25

26

27

28

29

PEQUENO JARDIM

CARLOS A. DOS SANTOS

FLORES E PLANTAS NATURAIS

30

31

32

33

34

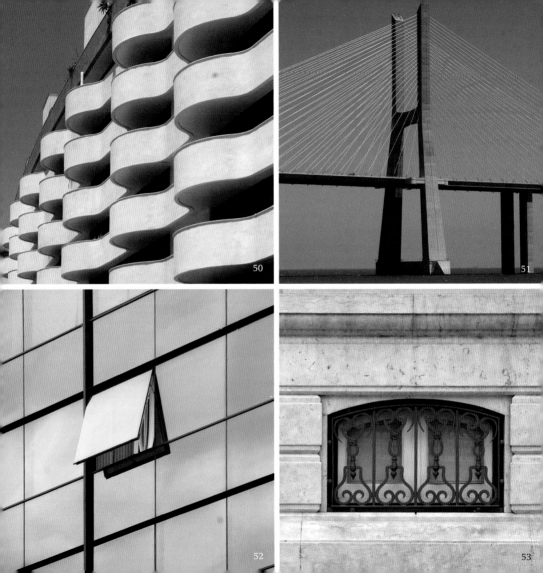

50

51

52

53

54

55

56

57

58

59

64

65

66

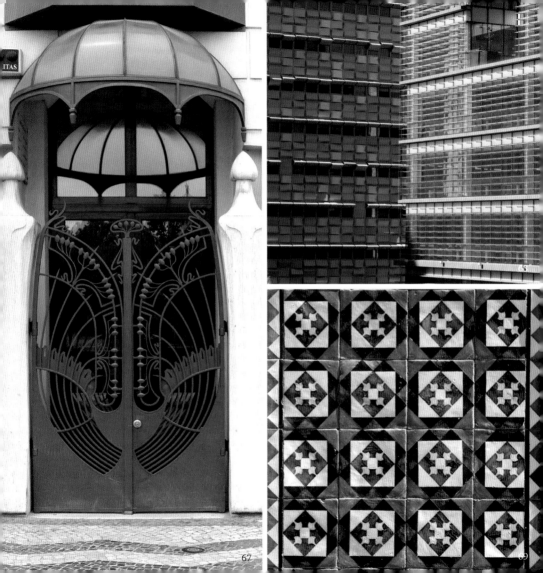

67

69

70

71

72

77

78

79

80

81

82

83

84

85

86

87

88

89

90

LJUBLJANA

The capital of Slovenia is marked in both its architecture and its culture by its centuries under Habsburg rule and by the tumultuous events of the 20th century. Today, the beautifully preserved old town is its main tourist magnet, with its fortress, town hall, bridges, promenades, colonnades and markets.

La capitale de la Slovénie est toujours marquée par des siècles sous la domination des Habsbourgs et puis les événements tumultueux du XXe siècle, dont les influences sont visibles dans la culture ainsi que l'architecture de la ville. Aujourd'hui, la vieille ville est un grand centre touristique, dont la forteresse, la mairie, les ponts, les promenades, les marchés et les colonnades sont merveilleusement conservés.

Sloweniens Hauptstadt ist architektonisch wie kulturell von der jahrhundertelangen Zugehörigkeit zum Habsburgerreich und ihrer bewegten Geschichte im 20. Jahrhundert geprägt. Die wunderbar erhaltene Altstadt mit Burg und Rathaus, Brücken, Promenaden, Kolonnaden und Märkten ist heute ein Touristikmagnet.

15

16

17

18

19

20

21

26

27

28

29

30

31

32

41

42

43

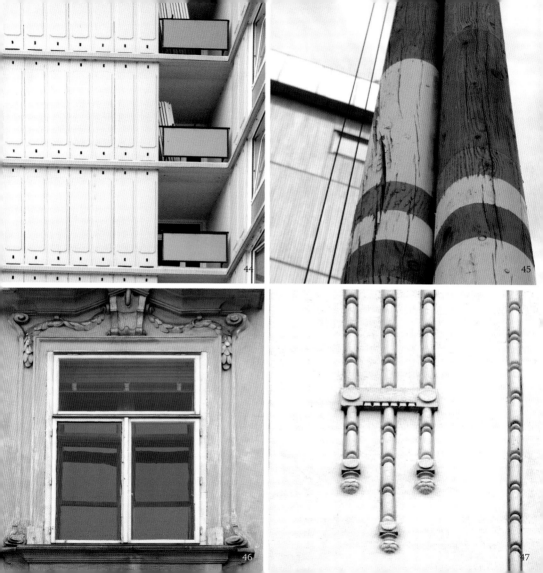

44

45

46

47

52

53

54

55

56

57

58

59

60

61

62

63

64

65

66

67

68

SREDNJA ŠOLA ZA ELEKTROTEHNIKO IN RAČUNALNIŠTVO

LJUBLJANA · VEGOVA 4

69

70

71

LONDON

The former center of the British empire features some of
Europe's most renowned buildings and palaces. It also famous
for its shopping streets. In London, history and modernity inter-
sect without much agitation, in typical British fashion. The EU's
most heavily populated city brings together countless delightful
traditions.

L'ancien centre de l'Empire britannique contient toujours
certains des bâtiments et des palais les plus célèbres de l'Europe,
ainsi que des grands magasins de renommée internationale. À
Londres, l'histoire et la modernité se croisent sans trop d'agitation, de façon typiquement brittanique. La ville la plus peuplée
de l'Europe regroupe de nombreuses traditions charmantes.

Das alte Zentrum des Empire besitzt einige der markantesten
und bekanntesten Bauwerke und Paläste Europas. Historie
und Moderne gehen hier eine sehr britische, unaufgeregte
Verbindung ein; berühmt sind auch die Shoppingmeilen. Die
bevölkerungsreichste Stadt der EU pflegt zahlreiche liebenswerte
Traditionen.

BUTLERS WHARF WEST

5

6

Lillywhites

7

13

14

15

16

17

18

19

20

21

22

23

24

25

26

35

36

IA FOSSA

37

38

50

51

52

53

54

55

56

REGENT gifts

61

62

NOTTING HILL
2
HOTEL

63

64

65

66

67

68

69

70

71

72

73

74

75

80

81

82

83

84

85

Judy Fox Antiques

PARIS

Paris has always been synonymous with elegance, modernity, and city life; its squares, streets, and boulevards stand testament to eras of centralized city planning. The Parisian way of life is reflected in its numerous cafés and galleries, a lively art scene, and extravagant buildings – the true face of a "Grande Nation".

Paris a toujours été synonyme d'élégance, de modernité et de vie urbaine. Ses places, ses rues et ses boulevards témoignent tous des époques de planification urbaine. Les nombreux cafés, les galeries, la scène artistique branchée et les bâtiments extravagants font tous partie du style de vie Parisien – la fameuse image de « la Grande Nation. »

Paris war immer schon das Synonym für Großstadt, Modernität und Eleganz; an ihren Plätzen, Straßen und Boulevards erkennt man die zentralistische Stadtplanung durch alle Epochen. Pariser Lebensart sind Straßencafés, Galerien, eine lebendige Kunstszene und extravagante Bauwerke – das Selbstbild einer „Grande Nation".

13

14

15

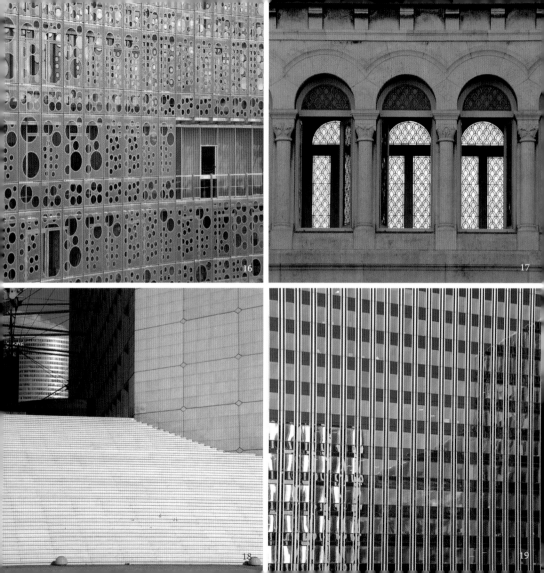

29

30

31

36

37

38

39

40

41

42

43

44

45

46

47

48

49

50

51

52

53

54

55

56

61

62

63

64

65

66

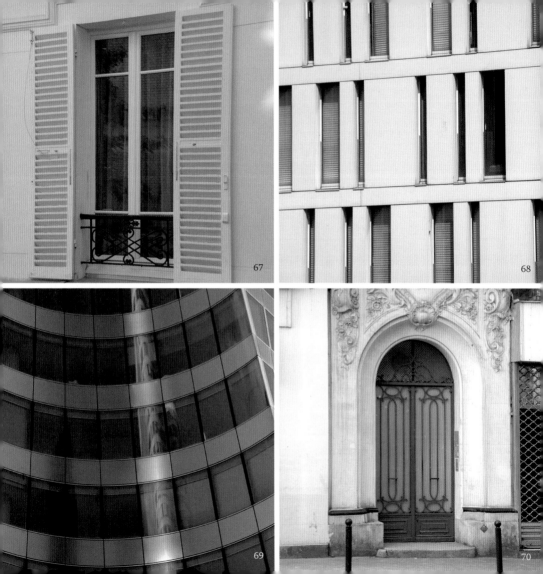

67

68

69

70

DX TOURS DE NOTRE D

71

72

73

74

75

76

77

78

79

80

PRAHA

The oldest university city in Europe, built the banks of the Vltava river, Prague was the cultural capital of Central Europe in the late Middle Ages, and again in 1600, before becoming its literary center. There are still a lot of hidden secrets to discover in Prague, such as its historic Jewish heritage, or the traces of Prague's own court artists, astronomers, and occultists.

La plus vieille ville universitaire de l'Europe, construite sur la rive de la Vltava, Prague était la capital culturelle de l'Europe Centrale jusqu'à la fin du Moyen-Âge et puis de nouveau en 1600, avant de devenir un centre littéraire. Il y a toujours plein de secrets à découvrir, comme son grand patrimoine juif ou bien les traces de ses artistes de cour, ses astronomes et ses occultistes.

Die an der Moldau gelegene älteste Universitätsstadt Europas war im Spätmittelalter und noch einmal um 1600 das kulturelle Zentrum Mitteleuropas, später die Stadt der Literaten. Bis heute gibt es hier viel Geheimnisvolles zu erkunden, etwa das alte jüdische Leben oder die Orte der hier tätig gewesenen Hofkünstler, Astronomen und Okkultisten.

5

6

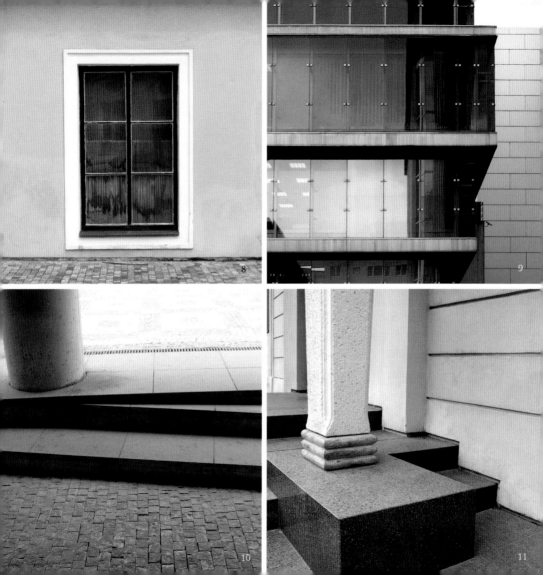

8

9

10

11

24

25

26

27

28

29

30

38

39

40

41

42

43

44

45

46

47

48

49

50

51

52

53

54

55

56

57

58

59

60

61

62

63

64

65

66

75

76

77

78

79

80

81

82

83

RIGA

Riga, the largest city in the Baltics, was a bone of contention between the Swedish, the Russians, and the Teutonic Order, and traces of this conflict can still be felt today. The well-preserved buildings in the historic town center are complemented by the Art Nouveau in the new districts. Today, Riga proudly proves its cultural independence.

La plus grosse ville de la Baltique témoigne toujours du conflit entre les Russes, les Suèdes et l'ordre teutonique. L'Art Nouveau des nouveaux quartiers s'accorde avec les anciens bâtiments de la vieille ville. Aujourd'hui, Riga montre fièrement son indépendance culturelle.

Die größte Stadt des Baltikums war lange ein Zankapfel zwischen Deutschem Orden, Schweden und Russen, was seine Spuren hinterließ. Die gut erhaltenen Bauten der historischen Altstadt werden von der Neustadt im Jugendstil ergänzt. Heute demonstriert Riga seine kulturelle Eigenständigkeit.

1

2

3

4

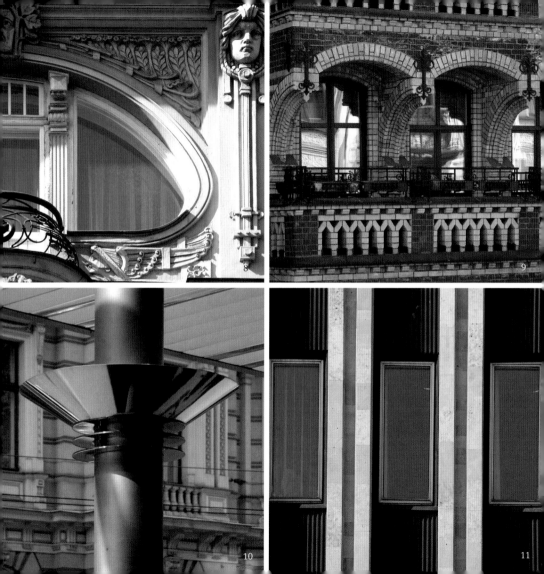

16

17

18

19

20

21

22

23

24

25

26

27

28

29

30

Tirgoņu iela

31

32

33

38

39

40

41

42

43

44

45

46

47

48

49

50

55

56

57

58

59

60

61

62

63

64

69

70

71

72

73

74

75

76

77

78

79

80

81

ROMA

This city, with its colossal monuments built on seven hills along the Tiber river, long held the title of "Caput Mundi" – capital of the world – first as the center of the Roman Empire, then as the seat of the Pope (in the Vatican). This legacy still shapes Rome's image today – no other city boasts as many celebrated buildings in such tight space.

Cette ville, construite sur sept collines au long du Tibre, était connue auparavant sous le nom de « Caput Mundi » - capitale du monde, d'abord en tant que capitale de l'Empire romain, et puis grâce au Saint-Siège (Vatican) de l'Église catholique. Cet héritage est toujours évident à Rome – aucune autre ville n'a autant de bâtiments renommés dans un espace si étroit.

Die auf sieben Hügeln am Tiber erbaute Stadt mit ihren kolossa-len Bauten war lange „Caput Mundi" – Haupt der Welt, erst als Mittelpunkt des Römischen Weltreiches, dann der Kirche als Sitz des Papstes (Vatikan). Dieses Erbe prägt das Selbstbewusstsein der Römer bis heute; wohl keine andere Stadt besitzt so viele berühmte Bauwerke auf engstem Raum.

5

6

7

23

24

25

26

27

28

29

30

31

32

33

34

35

36

37

38

39

40

41

42

43

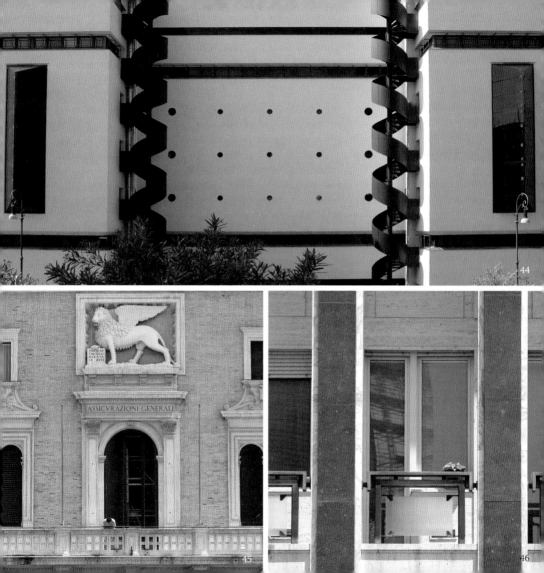

44

45

ASSICVRAZIONI GENERALI

46

55

56

57

58

59

60

61

66

67

PALAZZO DEI CONGR

68

69

70

71

72

77

78

79

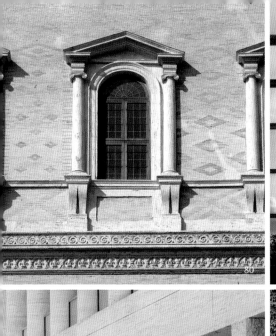

80

81

82

83

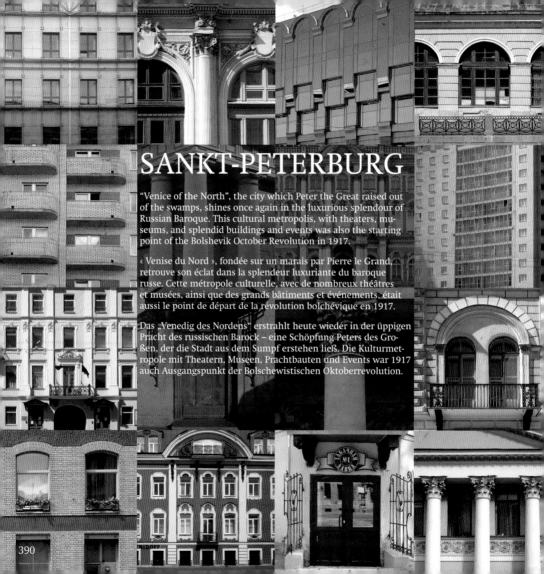

SANKT-PETERBURG

"Venice of the North", the city which Peter the Great raised out of the swamps, shines once again in the luxurious splendour of Russian Baroque. This cultural metropolis, with theaters, museums, and splendid buildings and events was also the starting point of the Bolshevik October Revolution in 1917.

« Venise du Nord », fondée sur un marais par Pierre le Grand, retrouve son éclat dans la splendeur luxuriante du baroque russe. Cette métropole culturelle, avec de nombreux théâtres et musées, ainsi que des grands bâtiments et événements, était aussi le point de départ de la révolution bolchévique en 1917.

Das „Venedig des Nordens" erstrahlt heute wieder in der üppigen Pracht des russischen Barock – eine Schöpfung Peters des Großen, der die Stadt aus dem Sumpf erstehen ließ. Die Kulturmetropole mit Theatern, Museen, Prachtbauten und Events war 1917 auch Ausgangspunkt der Bolschewistischen Oktoberrevolution.

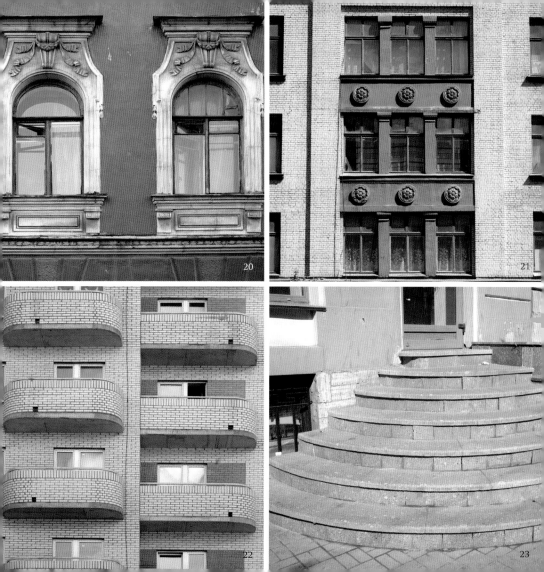

28

29

30

31

32

33

38

39

40

44

45

46

47

48

49

50

51

56

57

58

59

60

61

66

67

68

69

70

71

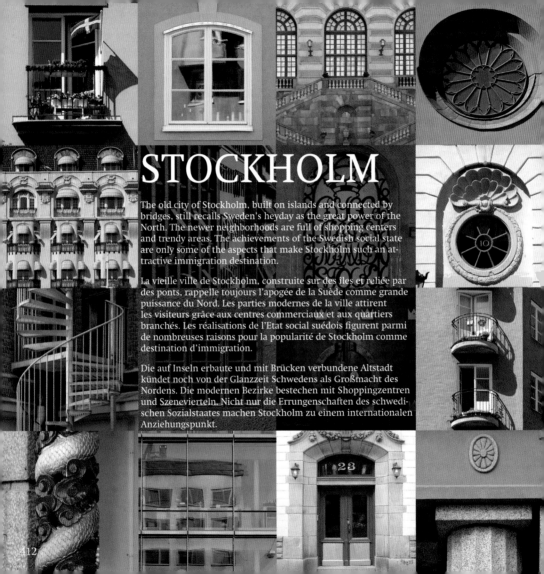

STOCKHOLM

The old city of Stockholm, built on islands and connected by bridges, still recalls Sweden's heyday as the great power of the North. The newer neighborhoods are full of shopping centers and trendy areas. The achievements of the Swedish social state are only some of the aspects that make Stockholm such an attractive immigration destination.

La vieille ville de Stockholm, construite sur des îles et reliée par des ponts, rappelle toujours l'apogée de la Suède comme grande puissance du Nord. Les parties modernes de la ville attirent les visiteurs grâce aux centres commerciaux et aux quartiers branchés. Les réalisations de l'Etat social suédois figurent parmi de nombreuses raisons pour la popularité de Stockholm comme destination d'immigration.

Die auf Inseln erbaute und mit Brücken verbundene Altstadt kündet noch von der Glanzzeit Schwedens als Großmacht des Nordens. Die modernen Bezirke bestechen mit Shoppingzentren und Szenevierteln. Nicht nur die Errungenschaften des schwedischen Sozialstaates machen Stockholm zu einem internationalen Anziehungspunkt.

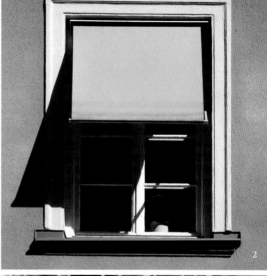

9

10

11

23

24

25

26

27

28

29

30

31

32

33

34

35

36

41

42

43

44

49

50

51

52

53

54

55

56

57

58

59

60

61

62

63

64

65

66

67

68

69

70

71

ARKITEKTU

72

73

79

80

81

82

83

84

85

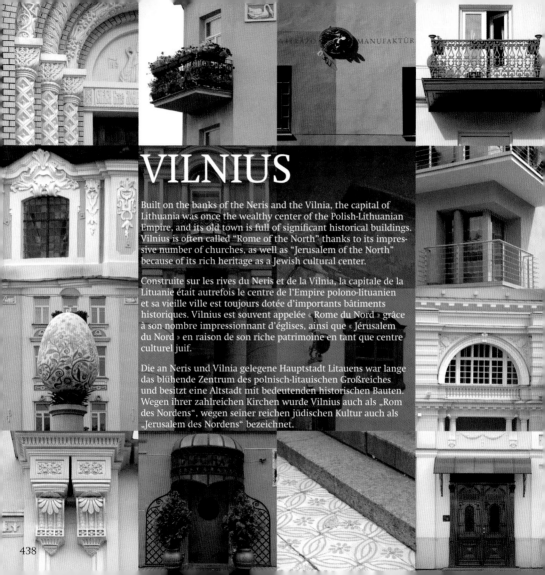

VILNIUS

Built on the banks of the Neris and the Vilnia, the capital of Lithuania was once the wealthy center of the Polish-Lithuanian Empire, and its old town is full of significant historical buildings. Vilnius is often called "Rome of the North" thanks to its impressive number of churches, as well as "Jerusalem of the North" because of its rich heritage as a Jewish cultural center.

Construite sur les rives du Neris et de la Vilnia, la capitale de la Lituanie était autrefois le centre de l'Empire polono-lituanien et sa vieille ville est toujours dotée d'importants bâtiments historiques. Vilnius est souvent appelée « Rome du Nord » grâce à son nombre impressionnant d'églises, ainsi que « Jérusalem du Nord » en raison de son riche patrimoine en tant que centre culturel juif.

Die an Neris und Vilnia gelegene Hauptstadt Litauens war lange das blühende Zentrum des polnisch-litauischen Großreiches und besitzt eine Altstadt mit bedeutenden historischen Bauten. Wegen ihrer zahlreichen Kirchen wurde Vilnius auch als „Rom des Nordens", wegen seiner reichen jüdischen Kultur auch als „Jerusalem des Nordens" bezeichnet.

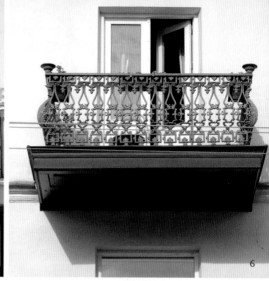

MUZIEJUS DIRBA
MUSEUM IS OPEN
10-17

12

13

14

15

16

17

18

19

20

21

22

24

25

26

35

36

37

38

39

40

41

42

43

44

45

46

47

48

49

50

55

56

57

60

61

62

63

64

65

66

UNIVERSITETO BIBLIOTEKA

PIRMAJAI LIETUVIŠKAI KNYGAI 1547—1997

WIEN

This charming and beautiful city vied with Paris to become the main residence of the Habsburg Emperor, and in 1900, it became the center of the artistic Avant-Garde (Viennese Modernism). Vienna is as famous for its café culture and Heuriger wine taverns as for its Prater leisure park.

À l'époque, Vienne rivalisait avec Paris pour devenir la résidence principale de l'empereur Habsbourg, et en 1900, elle devint le centre de l'avant-garde artistique (le modernisme viennois). Aujourd'hui, Vienne est aussi célèbre pour ses cafés et ses tavernes que pour son parc de loisirs, le Prater.

Die charmante und liebenswerte Stadt wetteiferte als Residenz der Habsburgerkaiser lange mit Paris und war um 1900 das Zentrum einer künstlerischen Avantgarde („Wiener Moderne"). Wien ist für seine Kaffeehaus-Kultur und gemütlichen Heurigen-Lokale ebenso berühmt wie für den Vergnügungspark Prater.

13

14

15

16

17

18

19

20

21

22

30

31

32

33

34

35

36

41

42

43

48

49

50

51

52

53

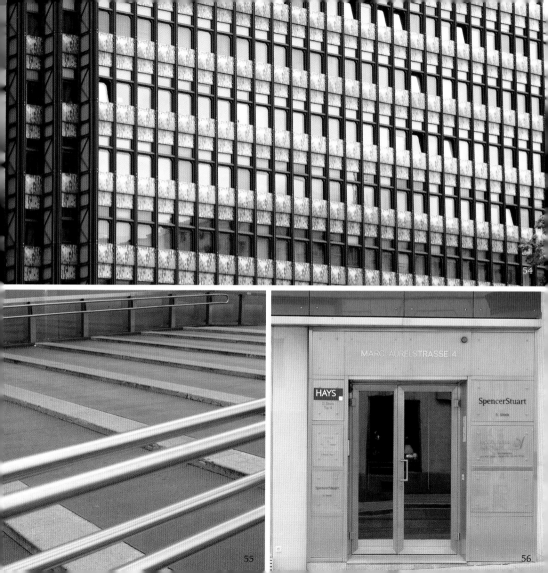

54

55

56

57

unsere Liebe deckte, das Riesenrad

58

59

60

61

62

63

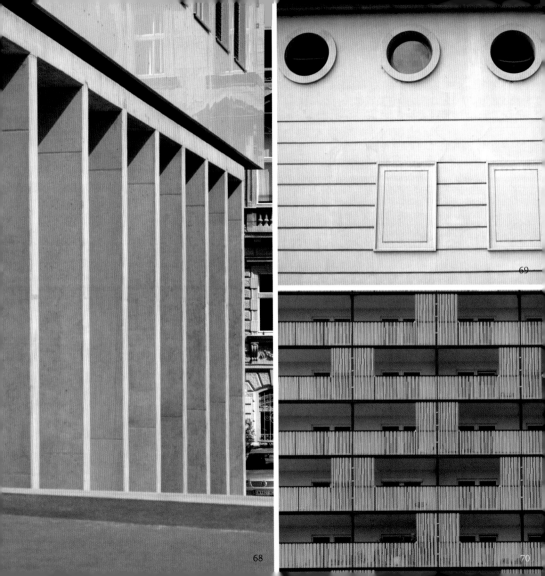

68

69

70

71

72

73

74

ZÜRICH

The buildings of the picturesque old town, built along the Limmat river, remind visitors both of the culture of federal freedom, and that this city was one of the centers of the Protestant Reformation. The center of town remains unchanged since the 19th century, while modern Zurich grows all around it.

Les bâtiments de la vieille ville de Zurich, construits le long de la Limmat, rappellent aux visiteurs la culture de la liberté du gouvernement fédéral et aussi que cette ville était l'un des centres de la Réforme protestante. Le centre de la ville n'a pas changé depuis le XIXe siècle, tandis que Zurich continue à s'étendre tout autour.

Die malerische Altstadt an der Limmat kündet mit ihren Bauten von der Bürgerkultur eidgenössischer Freiheiten sowie davon, dass die Stadt ein Zentrum der Reformation war. Ihr Stadtbild blieb erhalten, weil das moderne Zürich seit dem 19. Jahrhundert rund um die Altstadt herum erbaut wurde und wird.

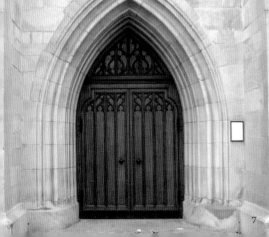

9

10

11

13

14

15

16

21

22

23

24

25

26

27

28

29

30

31

32

33

38

39

40

RANT ZUNFTHAUS ZUR WAAG

Check-in 3

41

42

43

44

45

46

47

48

49

50

51

52

53

54

59

60

61

62

BURGER

42

63

64

65

66

67

68

69

70

71

72

73

74

40

75

76

77

78

79

80

INDEX

marquès comillas 6–8 | 36 plaça d'espanya 6–8 | 37 paseo de gracia 92 (casa milà) | 38 paseo de gracia 92 | 39 calle mallorca 401 (sagrada família) | 40 calle mallorca 401 (sagrada família) | 41 passeig de gràcia 82 | 42 moll d'espanya 5–2 planta | 43 calle mallorca 401 | 44 avenida marquès de comillas 13 | 45 avenida marquès de comillas 13 | 46 marina 14–16 | 47 carrer d'olot (parc güell) | 48 via laietana 5 | 49 rambla del poblenou 125–127 | 50 calle mallorca 401 | 51 rambla de sant josep 55 | 52 gran via de les cortes catalanes 601 | 53 rambla de sant josep 51–59 | 54 avenida marquès de comillas 13 | 55 plaza del tibidabo 1 (temple expiatorio de sagrat cor) | 56 plaza del tibidabo 1 (temple expiatorio de sagrat cor) | 57 avenida marquès de comillas 13 | 58 gran via de les cortes catalanes 601 | 59 avenida marquès de comillas 92 | 60 avenida marquès de comillas 6–8 | 61 avenida de la cathédrale | 62 palacio del mar | 63 carrer d'olot (parc güell) | 64 via laietana 20 | 65 passeig de gràcia 66 | 66 avenida marquès de comillas 6–8 | 67 carrer d'aragó | 68 plaza del rei 2 (palau reial) | 69 carrer d'olot (parc güell) | 70 plaza del tibidabo 1 | 71 plaza del tibidabo 1 | 72 paseo de gracia 35 | 73 avenida marquès de comillas 13 | 74 avenida marquès de comillas 13 | 75 gran via de les cortes catalanes 606 | 76 avenida marquès de comillas | 77 calle mallorca 401 (sagrada família) | 78 plaza reial del rei 2 (palau reial) | 79 paseo de gracia 92 | 80 avenida marquès de comillas 13 | 81 avenida de la cathedral | 82 avenida marquès de comillas | 83 passeig de gracia 66 | 84 avenida marquès de comillas 13 | 85 avenida marquès de comillas 13 | 86 passeig de grácia 54 | 87 avenida marquès de comillas 13 | 88 calle mallorca 401 (sagrada família) | 89 rambla de sant josep 35

BERLIN

01 marlene-dietrich-platz 2 | 02 sony center | 03 strausberger platz | 04 spandauer damm 88 | 05 rykestraße 13 | 06 linkstraße 8–10 | 07 paul-löbe-allee | 08 stralauer platz 34 | 09 linkstraße 12 | 10 potsdamer platz | 11 hinter dem zeughaus 1 | 12 potsdamer straße 33 | 13 choriner straße 2 | 14 friedrich-list-ufer | 15 markgrafenstraße 43 | 16 hinter dem gießhaus/ unter den linden 2 | 17 unter den linden 2 | 18 bellevue straße/ henriette-hausner-straße | 19 wilhelmstraße 140 | 20 karl-marx-allee 33 | 21 hiroshimastraße 12–16 | 22 reichpietschstraße 60 | 23 pariser platz 6 | 24 charlottenstraße 44 | 25 reichtagsufer | 26 kochstraße 22 | 27 linkstraße 10 | 28 schiffbauerdamm | 29 besselstraße 4 | 30 augustraße 26a | 31 gendarmenmarkt | 32 hiroshimastraße 18 | 33 klingelhöferstraße 18 | 34 herbert-von-karajan-straße 1 | 35 händelallee (kaiser-friedrich-gedächtnis-kirche) | 36 klingelhöferstraße | 37 rauchstraße 1 | 38 unter den linden 4 | 39 cora-berliner-straße | 40 wilhelmstraße 124 | 41 hiroshimastraße 124 | 42 hiroshimastraße 17 | 43 hiroshimastraße 12–16 | 44 zimmerstraße 19/19a | 45 klingelhöferstraße 46 | 46 markgrafenstraße 46 | 47 linkstraße 10 | 48 behrenstraße 74 | 49 linkstraße 10 | 50 sony center | 51 willy-brandt-straße 1 | 52 am park 4 | 53 weydemeyer straße | 54 stralauer platz 34 | 55 christburger straße 26 | 56 zimmerstraße 19/19a | 57 lindenstraße 9–14 | 58 platz der vereinten nationen | 59 reichtagsufer | 60 karl-marx-allee 84 | 61 alt-moabit 143–145 | 62 stresemannstraße 60 | 63 cora-berliner-straße | 64 marlene-dietrich-platz | 65 herbert-von-karajan straße 1 | 66 invalidenstraße 50–51 | 67 potsdamer platz 11 / linkstraße 10 | 68 potsdamer platz | 69 hinter dem gießhaus/ unter den linden 2 | 70 alt-moabit 143–145 | 71 hinter dem gießhaus | 72 bruder-grimm-gasse 1 | 73 christburger straße 5 | 74 köthener straße 40 | 75 pariser platz 6 | 76 unter den linden 72 | 77 am friedrichshain 34 | 78 leipziger straße 43, 44 | 79 mittelstraße 2–4 | 80 hedemannstraße 4–6 | 81 zimmerstraße 100 | 82 welserstraße 2 | 83 lindenstraße 9–14 | 84 in den ministergärten | 85 schiffsbauerdamm | 86 rykestraße | 87 marlene-dietrich-platz | 88 behrenstraße 40–41 | 89 sony center

BRUXELLES

01 29, rue archimède | 02 4, rue du lycée | 03 parlament européen | 04 14, avenue palmerstrom | 05 sinter-goedeleplein | 06 parlement européen | 07 157, rue royale | 08 rue de bériot | 09 200, rue de la loi | 10 colline du congress III | 11 rue du marché-aux-herbes | 12 rue de la loi | 13 avenue galilée 1 | 14 1, greepstraat | 15 rue de la revolution iv | 16 107, rue albert | 17 place sainte-godule | 18 rue de rivoli | 19 80, rue belliard | 20 3, rue de Bordeaux | 21 rue wiertz (parlement européen) | 22 52, avenue des arts | 23 place de la bourse | 24 1. rue félix delhasse | 25 rue wiertz (parlement européen | 26 rue du brabant | 27 quartier léopold | 28 rue royale | 29 parc du cinquantenaire | 30 rue arthur diderich | 31 quartier léopold | 32 12, quai aux briques | 33 rue belliard 89 | 34 avenue paul henri spaak | 35 parlement européen | 36 17, boulevard baudouin | 37 48, rue de la croix de pierre | 38 rue du progress | 39 rue de france 42 | 40 204, rue royale | 41 parc léopold | 42 rue de la loi 133 | 43 16, quai aux briques | 44 2, rue de la banque | 45 rue du taciturne 1, | 46 boulevard de saint-lazare | 47 38, chaussée de wavre| 48 rue de boiteaux | 49 robert schumenplein | 50 boulevard anspach 23 | 51 boulevard du roi albert II | 52 36, rue du portugal | 53 22, grasmarkt | 54 place madou |

55 rue de la loi | 56 parlement européen | 57 grand place | 58 berlaymont | 59 chaussée d'anvers | 60 rue de la banque 2 | 61 12, avenue des gaulois | 62 rue wiertz | 63 avenune galilée | 64 grand place | 65 quartier léopold | 66 parlement européen | 67 29 rue vautier | 68 36 rue de la bourse | 69 rue du cirque | 70 conseil européen

BUDAPEST

01 sondi utca 6 | 02 nyugati tér | 03 dísz tér 15 | 04 szabadság tér 6 | 05 szabadság tér 6 | 06 rumbach sebestyén utca 6 | 07 milenáris park | 08 puskás ferenc stadion | 09 fortuna utca 6 | 10 metro blaha lujza tér | 11 mücsarnok | 12 millenáris park | 13 csaba utca 5 | 14 deák ferenc utca 12 | 15 budaer burg (magyar nemzeti galeria) | 16 halászbástya | 17 várfok utca 15b | 18 dózsa györgy utca 84b | 19 déak ferenc utca | 20 nyugati tér | 21 szabadság tér 15 | 22 szabadság tér 2 | 23 stefánia utca 14 | 24 állatkerti krt. 6–12 | 25 stefánia utca 2 | 26 városligeti farso 50 | 27 dísz tér 15 | 28 pasareti tér 14 | 29 palais sándor 10 | 30 stefánia utca | 31 déak ferenc utca 12 | 32 dózsa györgy utca 37 | 33 roosevelt tér | 34 honvéd utca 3 | 35 nemzeti színház | 36 pobrezni 1 | 37 dózsa györy utca 84a | 38 honvéd utca 3 | 39 gellért bath | 40 sándor utca | 41 deák ferenc utca 17 | 42 ajtósi dürer sor 37 | 43 csaba uca 5 | 44 bajcsy zsilinszky utca 12 | 45 vajdahunyadvára | 46 déak ferenc utca 11 | 47 halászbástya | 48 ditró utca 6 | 49 ferenciek tere 10 | 50 gellért bath | 51 halászbástya | 52 honvéd utca 3 | 53 ix. üllöi út 33–37 (iparmüvészeti museum) | 54 roosevelt tér 4 | 55 millenáris park 35 | 56 napraforgó utca 3 | 57 paulay ede utca 35 | 58 uri utca 17 | 59 szechenyi bad 12 | 60 stefánia utca 2 | 61 napraforgó utca 9 | 62 nagy zsinagóga | 63 nemzeti színház | 64 roosevelt tér 2 | 65 ix. bajor gizi park 1 | 66 mücsarnok | 67 lánchíd utca 19 | 68 hess andras ter 1–3 | 69 honvéd utca 3 | 70 roosevelt tér 2 | 71 király utca 74 | 72 király utca 74 | 73 markó utca 72 | 74 országház utca 22 | 75 ix. üllöi út 33–37 (iparmüvészeti museum) | 76 karoly körut 5 | 77 ferenciek tere 10 | 78 alsó rakpart | 79 napraforgó utca 2 | 80 nemzeti színház | 81 mücsarnok | 82 magyar nemzeti galleria | 83 paulay ede utca 35 | 84 nagy zsinagóga | 85 dísz tér 15 | 86 deák ferenc utca 19 | 87 lánchíd utca | 88 dohány utca 2 (nagy zsinagóga) | 89 millenáris park | 90 roosevelt tér | 91 honvéd utca 3 | 92 metro stadionok

HELSINKI

01 mannerheimaukio | 02 hammarskjöldintie | 03 korkeavuorenkatu | 04 rauhankatu | 05 itainenpapinkatu | 06 korkeavuorenkatu | 07 johnstenberginrata | 08 korkeavuorenkatu | 09 runeberginkatu | 10 runeberginkatu | 11 mannerheimintie | 12 korkeavuoren-katu | 13 intainenpapinkatu | 14 mannerheimintie | 15 aleksanterinkatu | 16 hallituskatu | 17 aleksanterinkatu | 18 läntinen teatte-rikuja | 19 kaivokatu | 20 mechelinkatu | 21 pohjoisesplanadin | 22 thakontie | 23 mannerheimintie | 24 mannerheimaukio | 25 mannerheimintie | 26 korkeavuorenkatu | 27 itainenpapinkatu | 28 mannerheimaukio | 29 abrahaminkatu | 30 läntinen teatterikuja | 31 mannerheimaukio | 32 kaivokatu | 33 eteläesplanade | 34 itainenpapinkatu | 35 abrahaminkatu | 36 hakaniemen-torikatu | 37 etaläinen rautatiekatu | 38 mannerheimintie | 39 unioninkatu | 40 ratakatu | 41 doebelninkatu | 42 aleksanterinkatu | 43 runeberginkatu 14 (helsinki school of economics) | 44 keskuskatu | 45 kaivokatu | 46 pohjrautatiekatu | 47 runeberginkatu | 48 pohjoisesplanadi | 49 ratakatu | 50 ratakatu | 51 eteläesplanade | 52 snellmaninkatu | 53 eteläinen rautatiekatu | 54 ratakatu | 55 hallituskatu | 56 korkeavuorenkatu | 57 erottajankatu | 58 etelaeinenrautatiekatu | 59 pohjoisesplanadin | 60 hammarskjöldintie

ISTANBUL

01 besiktas (topkapi sarayi) | 02 istikla caddesi | 03 soğuk çesme sokak | 04 besiktas (topkapi sarayi) | 05 kemankes caddesi | 06 istiklal caddesi | 07 ayşe kadın hamamı sokak | 08 dolmabahçe sarayi | 09 topkapi sarayi | 10 prof k.i. gurkan caddesi | 11 çıragan caddesi/ çıragan sarayi | 12 besitkas (dolmabahçe sarayi) | 13 taksim meydan | 14 sultan ahmed camii | 15 abdullahağa caddesi | 16 h'davendiga caddesi | 17 çırağan caddesi | 18 istiklal caddesi | 19 aya sofya | 20 sultan ahmed camii | 21 divanyolu caddesi | 22 alay köşkü | 23 kazim ismail gürkan caddesi | 24 prof k.i. gurkan caddesi | 25 sultan ahmet camii | 26 besiktas (dolmabahçe sarayi) | 27 istiklal caddesi | 28 dolmabahçe sarayi | 29 h'davendiyar caddesi | 30 kemeralti caddesi | 31 tavukhane sokak | 32 mescutiyet caddesi | 33 tavukhane sokak | 34 besiktas (dolmabahçe sarayi) | 35 dolmabahçe sarayi | 36 cergefci sokak | 37 zeynep sultan sokak | 38 istiklal caddesi | 39 istiklal caddesi | 40 atmeydani sokak | 41 soğuk çesme sokak | 42 h'davendigar caddesi | 43 kennedy caddesi | 44 taksim meydan | 45 sultan ahmet camii | 46 soğuk çesme sokak | 47 ahmediye camii | 48 topkapi sarayi | 49

prof. kazim ismail gürkan caddesi | 50 ayse kadın hammamı sokak | 51 soğuk çeşme sokak | 52 buyuk hendek caddesi | 53 divanyoluc caddesi | 54 dolmabahçe sarayi | 55 kuzguncuk çarsi caddesi | 56 soğuk çesme sokak | 57 h'davendigar caddesi | 58 aya sofya | 59 istiklal caddesi | 60 soğuk çesme sokak | 61 besiktas (dolmabahçe sarayi) | 62 divanyolu caddesi | 63 aya sofya | 64 dolmabahçe sarayi | 65 tavukhane sokak | 66 istiklal caddesi | 67 prof. kazim ismail gürkan caddesi | 68 tavukhane sokak | 69 prof. kazim ismail gürkan caddesi | 70 h'davendigar caddesi | 71 taksim meydan | 72 tavukhane sokak | 73 iskele caddesi | 74 küçük ayasofya caddesi/ tavukhane sokak | 75 topkapi sarayi

KRAKÓW

01 ulica św. gertrudy 3 | 02 rynek glówny 2 | 03 ulica wielopole | 04 ulica golebria | 05 aleja kasińskiego 18 | 06 maly rynek 8 | 07 os. centrum b15 | 08 plac kolejowy 1 | 09 ulica wielopole 6 | 10 aleja kasisskiego 1 | 11 rynek glówny 2 | 12 ulica starowislna | 13 ulica kopernika 16 | 14 ulica estery 18 | 15 plac kolejowy 1 | 16 plac na groblach 11 | 17 ulica wielopole 1 | 18 plac ducha 1 | 19 wzgórze wawelskie | 20 podzamcze 17 | 21 ulica spitalna 40 | 22 rynek glówny 4 | 23 ulica lubicz 1 | 24 wielopole 6 | 25 ulica straszewskiego 34 | 26 ulica śn gertrudy 12 | 27 ulica dunajewskiego 13 | 28 ulica marsz j. pilsudsiego 32 | 29 ulica meiselsa 22 | 30 rynek glówny 3 | 31 maly rynek 9 | 32 ulica ogrodowa 4 | 33 ulica św. gertrudy 3 | 34 uniwersytet | 35 konserwatorium | 36 ulica zwierzyniecka 30 | 37 kraków glówny | 38 plac szczepaĐski 3a | 39 kraków glówny | 40 ulica bernardýńka | 41 ulica meiselsa 23 | 42 ulica szewska | 43 ulica św gertrudy 67 | 44 plac jana nowaka jeziorańskiego | 45 smina 11 | 46 wawel | 47 plac nowy 23 | 48 ulica św. anny 2 | 49 ulica straszewskiego 34 | 50 plac nowy 23 | 51 ulica wielopo 2 | 52 wawel | 53 plac ducha 1 | 54 ulica jablonowskich 7 | 55 ulica powiĐle 12 | 56 ulica wielopole 1–3 | 57 ulica podwale | 58 ulica ogrodowa 4 | 59 ulica golebia | 60 ulica sienna | 61 ulica Đw. tomasza | 62 ulica westerplatte 34 | 63 kraków glówny | 64 ulica miodowa | 65 ulica radziwillowska 3 | 66 wawel | 67 rynek glówny | 68 plac nowy | 69 ulica wielopole 30

LISBOA

01 rua do jasmin | 02 rua castilho 50 | 03 azulejos | 04 praçá dom joão da câmara 5 | 05 igreja de santa maria | 06 avenida sidonio pais | 07 largo do chiado | 08 parque das nações | 09 parque das nações | 10 metro oriente | 11 rua marquês da fonteira | 12 parque das nações | 13 parque das nações | 14 rua do alecrim 26 | 15 rua do alecrim | 16 rua aurea 247 | 17 praçá do imperio | 18 rua nova da trindade 9 | 19 parque das nações | 20 azulejos | 21 avenida infante santo | 22 avenida da republica 38a | 23 parque das nações | 24 rua braamcamp 40 | 25 parque das nações | 26 rua dos fangueiros 106 | 27 rua augusta | 28 parque das nações | 29 rua do alecrim 20 | 30 rua garrett 60 | 31 rua da sandale 43 | 32 avenida da libertade | 33 avenida da república | 34 azulejos | 35 avenida fontes pereira de melo 10 | 36 avenida de liberdade 175 | 37 parque das nações | 38 avenida da república | 39 igraja de santa maria major | 40 metro oriente | 41 largo do regedor | 42 avenida da república 38a | 43 rua do arsenal | 44 parque des nações | 45 avenida infante santo | 46 parque das nações | 47 parque das nações | 48 parque das nações | 49 rua garrett 36 | 50 parque das naçôes | 51 parque das nações | 52 avenida fontes pereira de melo 13 | 53 avenida fontes pereira de melo | 54 rua da prata 81 | 55 parque das nações | 56 avenida infante santo | 57 avenida fontes pereira de melo | 58 rua dos bacalhoeiros 11 | 59 parque das naçôes | 60 pereira de malo 19 | 61 parque das nações | 62 parque das nações | 63 avenida da liberdade | 64 parque das nações | 65 avenida da república 37 | 66 avenida antónio augusto de aguiar 66 | 67 avenida da república | 68 parque des nações | 69 azulejos | 70 praçá dom loco da cama | 71 parque das nações | 72 parque das nações | 73 parque das nações | 74 parque das nações | 75 rua das portas de santo antão | 76 rua da palma | 77 rua garrett 81 | 78 parque das nações | 79 rua do alecrim | 80 avenida columbano bordelo pinheiro 55 | 81 avenida de la republica 87 | 82 praçá dom joão | 83 metro oriente | 84 travessa do saltra 80 | 85 parque das nações | 86 rua do alecrim 20 | 87 parque das nações| 88 parque das nações | 89 palacio da justiça | 90 azulejos

LJUBLJANA

01 hribarjevo nabrežje | 02 miklošičeva cesa 8 | 03 gradasjka ulica 20 | 04 mestni trg 4 | 05 kongresni trg 11 | 06 stritarjeva ulica 6 | 07 stritarjeva ulica 6 | 08 tabor 4 | 09 ribji trg | 10 trg republike 1 | 11 kongresni trg 11 | 12 riharjeva ulica 19 | 13 dalmatinova ulica 2 | 14 trg republike 1 | 15 stari trg 7 | 16 vodnikov trg | 17 stari trg 11a | 18 gosposka ulica 5 | 19 kongresni trg 10

(slovenska filharmonija) | 20 adamic-lundrovo nabrezje | 21 vodnikov trg 6 | 22 cankarjeva ulica 18 | 23 štefanova ulica 18 | 24 presernova cesta 24 | 25 riharveja ulica 17 | 26 tabor 4 | 27 zoisova ulica 12 | 28 rožna ulica | 30 miklošičeva cesta | 31 grudnovo nabcezje | 32 miklošičeva cesta 3 | 33 trg republike | 34 aškerčeva ulica 5 | 35 gosposka ulica 5 | 36 tabor 2 | 37 kopitarjeva ulica 2 | 38 stritarjeva ulica 6 | 39 cankarjeva cesta 15 (moderna galerija) | 40 riharjeva ulica 19 | 41 krakovska ulica 21 | 42 aškerčeva ulica 5 | 43 čopova ulica 3 | 44 tabor 9 (hotel park) | 45 poljanska cesta / kopitarjeva ulica | 46 gruberjeva palača | 47 univerza | 48 prešernov trg 5/6 | 49 dalmatinova ulica | 50 tabor 13 (športno društvo) | 51 zoisova ulica 12 | 52 cankarjevo nabrežje 27 | 53 hribarjevo nabrežje | 54 igriska ulica 3 | 55 slovenska ulica / števanova ulica (nebotičnik) | 56 rožna ulica | 57 aškerčeva ulica 5 | 58 trg republike | 59 riharjeva ulica 19 | 60 mestni trg 1 (rotovž) | 61 gerbejevo stopnisce | 62 zoisova ulica | 63 zupančičeva ulica 4 | 64 gruberjeva palača | 65 stari trg 34 | 66 tavčarjeva ulica 8a | 67 zupaničičeva ulica 1 (sng opera in balet ljubljana) | 68 cankarjeva ulica 16 | 69 resljeva cesa 15 | 70 vegova ulica 1 | 71 vegova ulica 1 | 72 karunova ulica 14a | 73 miklošičeva cesta 18 | 74 adamic-lundrovo nabrezji | 75 krakovska ulica 21

LONDON

01 49 chiswell street | 02 threadneedle street (bank of england) | 03 shad thames | 04 cromwell road | 05 29, st martin's road | 06 picadilly circus (criterion theatre) | 07 66 pont street | 08 25 pembridge road | 09 one canada square | 10 32 old compton street | 11 7 lothbury road | 12 lothbury court (bank of england) | 13 24 cornhill street | 14 tower bridge | 15 5 copper row | 16 south kensington campus (imperial college london) | 17 bankside | 18 covent garden market | 19 9–11 copper row | 20 133 victoria street (ashdown house) | 21 55 kensington high street | 22 covent garden market | 23 imperial college | 24 87–133 brompton road (harrods) | 25 city hall | 26 13 walter street/ ovington street | 27 79–81 euston road (st pancras) | 28 64–68 exhibition road | 29 123 victoria street (ashdown house) | 30 millenium bridge | 31 131–141 kings road | 32 58 chepstow villas | 33 kensington temple | 34 29 greek street | 35 28 old compton street (prince edward theatre) | 36 west india quay | 37 butler's wharf | 38 knightrider street | 39 28 shad thames, butler's wharf | 40 1 aldwych | 41 the queen's walk (city hall) | 42 st paul's churchyard | 43 parliament street | 44 20 burg street | 45 1 lime street (lloyds building) | 46 1 lime street (lloyds building) | 47 covent garden market | 48 st george's wharf (shad thames) | 49 tower bridge | 50 42 cornhill street | 51 bankside | 52 1 lime street | 53 tooley street | 54 buckingham palace | 55 st george's street | 56 london bridge walk | 57 st. martin's lane | 58 55 victoria street | 59 london bridge | 60 1 aldwych | 61 covent garden market | 62 87–135 brompton road (harrods) | 63 2 pembridge garden | 64 9 portobello road | 65 kensington court | 66 fulham road (brompton hospital) | 67 22 hertsmere road | 68 thames pass | 69 13 lincoln's inn fields | 70 101–111 kensington high street | 71 st george's wharf (shad thames) | 72 bankside | 73 chepstow villas | 74 33 cornhill street | 75 king's cross | 76 chepstow villas | 77 cromwell road | 78 1 lime street | 70 87–135 brompton road | 80 1 coleman street | 81 5 copper row | 82 bartholomew lane/ lothbury court | 83 covent garden market | 84 195–197 kings road | 85 114–113 walton street | 86 79/81 portobello road

PARIS

01 19 boulevard jourdan | 02 centre pompidou | 03 esplanade de la défense | 04 rue emile durkheim | 05 montmartre | 06 quai françois mauriac (bibliothèque nationale de france) | 07 9 rue des écoles | 08 4 place jussieu | 09 rue des abbesses/ rue andré antoine | 10 place du parvis (notre dame) | 11 parvis de la défense (église de notre dame de la pentecôte) | 12 14 rue sant-julien le pauvre | 13 esplanade de la défense | 14 esplanade de la défense | 15 34 quai louvre | 16 4 place jussieu | 17 35 rue du chevalier de la barre (basilique du sacré cœur de montmartre) | 18 parvis de la défense | 19 193 rue de bercy | 20 cour napoléon | 21 esplanade de la défense | 22 90 boulevard haussmann (galeries lafayettes) | 23 quai de la gare | 24 57 boulevard st-germain | 25 21 rue de lyon | 26 église de montmartre | 27 41–47 quai austerlitz | 28 20 rue royale | 29 parc de la coupoule | 30 louvre | 31 rue d bercy 223 | 32 223 rue de bercy | 33 39 rue de la bouchere | 34 esplanade de la défense | 35 27c boulevard jourdan (maison heinrich heine) | 36 esplanade de la défense | 37 esplanade de la défense | 38 9 rue danielle casanova | 39 1 rue des fossés saint-bernard | 40 1 rue azaïs | 41 4 place jussieu | 42 1 rue paul klee | 43 4 place jussieu | 44 19 boulevard jourdan | 45 421 rue de lyon | 46 place du panthéon | 47 rue des abbesses/ rue andré antoine | 48 rue tornon | 49 1 rue edmond flamand | 50 41–47 quai austerlitz | 51 place du parvis (notre-dame) | 52 rue des fossés saint-bernard | 53 4 place jussieu | 54 21 boulevard diderot | 55 13 rue des écoles | 56 esplanade de la défense | 57 rue grégoire de tour 33 | 58 boulevard de l'hôpital | 59 2 église de montmartre | 60 rue de mont cenis | 61 1 rue azaïs | 62 4 place jussieu | 63 esplanade de la défense | 64 centre pompidou | 65 8–20 rue raymond aron | 66 21 rue des

abbesses | 67 **5 rue gabrielle** | 68 **8–20 rue raymon aron** | 69 esplanade de la défense | 70 **47 rue berger** | 71 **2 rue des écoles** | 72 22 rue du cloître | 73 quai de la gare | 74 **82 boulevard st-germain** | 75 quai de la gare | 76 place de la coupole | 77 **1 rue des fossés saint-bernard** | 78 pont charles de gaulle / quai austerlitz | 79 place jussieu 4 | 80 **10 esplanade de la défense**

PRAHA

01 dušm 12 | 02 jungmann ulicka 31 | 03 pražský hrad | 04 na příkopě 20 | 05 arcibiskupský palác | 06 na příkopě 22 | 07 krácovská zahrada |08 u prašného mostu 3 | 09 vinohradská 10 | 10 radlicka 4 | 11 pražský hrad | 12 neklanova 30 | 13 rašínovo nábřeží | 14 pražský hrad | 15 radnicke schody | 16 rybna 20 | 17 masarykovo nábřežíz | 18 hradčanské náměstí 16 | 19 radlická 5 | 20 celetná 29 | 21 stroupežnického 21 | 22 pražský hrad | 23 hradčanské náměstí 5 | 24 mahlerovy sady 1 | 25 libustina 3 | 26 u prašného mostu 4 | 27 areál výstaviště 67 | 28 zlata ulicka 24 | 29 jungmannova | 30 u prašného mostu 3 | 31 náměstí curieovych 100 | 32 krácovská zahrada | 33 pražský hrad | 34 schwarzenbersky palác | 35 rasinovo nabrezi 80 | 36 jirska 3 | 37 pražský hrad | 38 zlata ulicka 25 | 39 radlická 1 | 40 hový svet 5 | 41 loretánské náměstí 5 | 42 pražský hrad | 43 koulova 15 | 44 kotva 7 | 45 karla englise 11 | 46 haštalská 4 | 47 průmyslový palác | 48 pražský hrad | 49 jirska 2 | 50 václavské náměstí 27 | 51 na příkopě 19 | 52 pražský hrad | 53 náměstí curieovych | 54 stroupežnického 21 | 55 u prašného mostu 1 | 56 zlata ulicka 25 | 57 stroupežnického 21 | 58 václavské náměstí 25 | 59 wilsonova 2 | 60 u prašného mostu 1 | 61 vinohradská 8 | 62 pražský hrad | 63 neklanova 30 | 64 loretánské náměstí 36 | 65 vácavské náměstí 36 | 66 rybná 20 | 67 škrétova 12 | 68 václavské náměstí 27 | 69 vikarska 4 | 70 na příkopě 15 | 71 zlata ulicka 25 | 72 nádražní 27 | 73 na příkopě | 74 vinohradska 8 | 75 ovocný trh 10 | 76 pražský hrad | 77 staromestske náměstí 1 | 78 pražský hrad | 79 koulova 15 | 80 pražský hrad | 81 na příkopě/ vaclávské náměstí 1 | 82 radnicke schody 2 | 83 pražský hrad

RIGA

01 piels ielā | 02 krišjāna valdemāra ielā | 03 kalpaka bulvāris | 04 pils ielā | 05 jurmala | 06 ganu ielā | 07 jurmala | 08 elisabetes ielā | 09 brieža ielā | 10 kalpaka bulvāris | 11 kalpaka bulvāris | 12 jurmala | 13 antonijas ielā | 14 jākaba ielā 11 | 15 brivibas bulvāris | 16 kalpaka bulvāris | 17 škūnu ielā | 18 reimersa ielā | 19 reimersa ielā | 20 2 tornu ielā | 21 valnu ielā | 22 alberta ielā 12a | 23 jurmala | 24 krišjāna valdemāra ielā (national museum of art) | 25 kronvalda bulvāris | 26 cementery brālu kapri | 27 kronvalda bulvāris 2 | 28 elisabetes ielā 55 | 29 gogola ielā | 30 elisabetes ielā 10b | 31 elisabetes ielā | 32 kipsala | 33 jurmala | 34 azenes ielā | 35 jurmala | 36 kepaka bulvāris | 37 strēlmieku ielā | 38 maza pils ielā 17–21 | 39 antonijas ielā | 40 ieriku ielā 10a | 41 elisabetes ielā 10a | 42 jurmala | 43 jākaba ielā | 44 baznicas ielā | 45 elisabetes ielā 23 | 46 pareizticigo katedrale | 47 citadela ielā | 48 pils laukums 4 | 49 krišjāna valdemāra | 50 teātra ielā | 51 arsenēla ielā | 52 lomonosova ielā | 53 kalpaka bulvāris | 54 jurmala | 55 brivibas ielā | 56 citadeles ielā | 57 pils ielā | 58 kipsala | 59 antonijas ielā | 60 bruninieku ielā | 61 kungu ielā | 62 elisabetes ielā 10b | 63 citadeles ielā | 64 kipsala | 65 medmieku ielā | 66 jurmala | 67 citadeles ielā | 68 kronvalda bulvāris | 69 elisabetes ielā 15 | 70 alberta ielā | 71 reimersa ielā | 72 strelnieku laukums 1 | 73 pils ielā | 74 pulkveža brieža ielā 12 | 75 jurmala | 76 pulkveža brieža ielā 18 | 77 kungu ielā 7 | 78 dzirnavu ielā | 79 jurmala | 80 elisabetes ielā | 81 krematorija

ROMA

01 via dei cerchi 75 | 02 via ruggero bonghi 36 | 03 foro romano | 04 via giulia 190 | 05 piazza san clemente trilussa 45 | 06 via ottaviano 18 | 07 piazzale dei santi pietro e paolo | 08 viale america 229 | 09 largo gaetano agnesi | 10 foro romano | 11 via di san teodoro 4 | 12 foro romano | 13 via di san teodoro | 14 san pietro in vaticano | 15 via di san teodoro | 16 piazza del colosseo | 17 via m. minghetti | 18 via bocca di leon 45 | 19 viale america 229 | 20 piazza del campidoglio | 21 foro romano | 22 viale dell' arte 13 | 23 piazza die cinquecento | 24 viale della civiltà del lavoro | 25 via sacra (foro romano) | 26 viale della civiltà del lavoro | 27 viale vaticano | 28 via angelo poliziano 61 | 29 via di san teodoro | 30 via ruggero bonghi 36 | 31 via labicana 144 | 32 foro romano | 33 viale dell' arte 44 | 34 via vespasiano 23 | 35 foro romano | 36 via della domus aurea/ giardini | 37 viale dell'arte | 38 via bocca di leon 42 | 39 viale dell'arte | 40 via di san teodoro 2 | 41 basilica di san pietro in vaticano | 42 via gregoriana 22 | 43 via vittorino da feltre | 44 via labicana 144 | 45 piazza venezia 11 | 46 viale america 359 | 47 via buonarroti 41 | 48 piazza colonna | 49 via gregoriana 12 | 50 via cristoforo colombo | 51 viale vaticano | 52 viale della civiltà del lavoro | 53 via po 8 | 54 piazzale degli archivi |

55 basilica di san pietro in vaticano | 56 viale america 229 | 57 via francesco giambullari | 58 via di san teodoro | 59 via ruggero bonghi | 60 via sacra | 61 via angelo poliziano 71 | 62 piazza farnèse | 63 viale america 311 | 64 piazza degli archivi | 65 via angelo poliziano | 66 via san giovanni in laterano 28 | 67 piazza john kennedy 1 | 68 viale della civiltà romana | 69 viale america 361 | 70 piazza della rotonda 116 | 71 piazza farnèse | 72 via dell'arte 19 | 73 viale della domus aurea 5 | 74 via buonarroti 41 | 75 via ludovico muratori 25 | 76 piazza del colosseo | 77 fontana di trevi | 78 viale della civiltà del lavoro | 79 via del poggio laurentino 2 | 80 piazza farnèse | 81 via pinciana 35 | 82 piazzale degli archivi | 83 via di san teodoro

SANKT-PETERBURG

01 ismailovski prospekt | 02 karavannnaja ul. 8 | 03 sovetski perenlok 1 | 04 malaja konjuschennaja ul. 5 | 05 isaakijevski sobor | 06 krasnoarmeijskaja ul. 13 | 07 bolschaja konjuschennaja ul. 13 | 08 nab. reki fontanki 66 | 09 nevskij prospekt 41 | 10 moskovski prospekt 161 | 11 italianski ul. 19 | 12 rossiiskaja natsionalnaja biblioteka | 13 nevskij prospekt 40 | 14 nab. reki moiki 3 | 15 kirotshnaja ul. 7 | 16 nab. reki fontanki 14 | 17 karavannaja ul. 10 | 18 ul. tschernyschevkogo 3 | 19 nab. reki moiki 3 | 20 ul. egorova 16 | 21 ul. warschavskaja 22 | 22 ul. warschavskaya 23 | 23 vladimirski prospekt | 24 bolschaja konjuschennaja ul. 5 | 25 rossiiskaja natsionalnaja biblioteka | 26 nab. reki moiki 15 | 27 nab. reki fontanki 82 | 28 nab. reki fontanki 8 | 29 ismailovski prospekt 3 | 30 vladimirski prospekt 19 | 31 ul. pestelja | 32 ul. warschavskaja 19 | 33 dumskaja ul. 4 | 34 nevskij prospekt (gastini dvor) | 35 ul. warschavskaja 23 | 36 ul. warschavskaja 23 | 37 italianksaja ul. | 38 nab. reki fontanki 123 | 39 moskovski prospekt 165 | 40 nevskij prospekt 66 | 41 dvortsovaia naberezhnaia 34 | 42 bolshaja morskaja ul. 3 | 43 sagorodnij prospekt 20 | 44 nevskij prospekt 54 | 45 malaja konjuschennaja ul. 7 | 46 vladimirski prospekt 19 | 47 bolschaja morskaja ul. | 48 bolschaja kojuschennaja ul. 15 | 49 dumskaja ul. | 50 nab. reki fontanki | 51 krasnoarmeijskaja ul. 12 | 52 vladimirski prospekt 2 | 53 kirotshnaja ul. 24 | 54 malaja konjuschennaja ul. 1 | 55 malaja konjuschennaja ul. 5 | 56 krasnoarmeijskaja ul. 7 | 57 nab. reki fontanki 31 | 58 nevskij prospekt 57 | 59 placu ostrowskiego | 60 italianskaja ul.4 | 61 karavannaja ul.10 | 62 vladimirski prospekt 19 | 63 klinski prospekt 15 | 64 nab. relo moiki | 65 italianskaja ul. 5 | 66 karavannaja ul. 2 | 67 malaja konjuschennaja ul. 5 | 68 vladimirski prospekt 19 | 69 glavnyi shtab | 70 moskovski prospekt 165 | 71 ul. gastello 9

STOCKHOLM

01 eriksbergsgatan 30 | 02 tegnérgatan | 03 drottninggatan | 04 kyrkogatan | 05 radmansgatan | 06 mäster samuelsgatan 9 | 07 drottninggatan 9 | 08 uggleviksgatan | 09 kocksgatan 41 | 10 gamla riksarkivet | 11 klippagatan 16 | 12 kungliga slottet | 13 döbelsgatan 20 | 14 olaf palmes gatan 15 | 15 riddarholmen | 16 linnégatan | 17 drottninggatan 33 | 18 birger jarlsgatan 77 | 19 nytorgsgatan | 20 stortoget | 21 nytorgsgatan | 22 tegnérgatan 41 | 23 rädmansgatan 35 | 24 sveavägen 36 | 25 ordenstrappen 3 | 26 tulegatan 15 | 27 bondegatan | 28 asögatan 174 | 29 drottninggatan 33 | 30 prästgatan | 31 kavarlägen 17 | 32 folkungagatan 46 | 33 jakobs torg | 34 drottninggatan 33 | 35 danderydsgatan 2 | 36 konsert huset | 37 kungsbron 21 | 38 klippagatan 18 | 39 birger jarls torg 1 | 40 strandvägen| 41 bondegatan 72 | 42 tegnérgatan 8| 43 engelbrektsgatan 37 | 44 liljeholmen | 45 tulegatan 6 | 46 stortoget 16 | 47 kungsbron 21 | 48 tulegatan 14 | 49 kungsgata| 50 stadshuset | 51 liljeholmen | 52 hantverkargatan | 53 asögaten 173 | 54 hotörget | 55 riddarholmen | 56 centralbron | 57 drottninggatan 33 | 58 riddarholmen (gamla riksarkivet) | 59 danderydsgatan 16 | 60 beckbrännasbacken 1 | 61 strandvägen 17 | 62 södra blasieholmshamnen | 63 danderydsgatan 11 | 64 danderydsgatan 17 | 65 trängsund 1 | 66 nötorget 8 (konserthuset) | 67 regeringsgatan 107 | 68 erisbergsgatan | 69 odergatan | 70 hamngatan 10 | 71 kocksgatan 18 | 72 östermalmsgatan 28 | 73 bondegatan 74 | 74 kungsträdgardsgatan 10 | 75 tulegatan 15 | 76 folkungsgatan 46b | 77 stortoget | 78 folkungatrappan | 79 drottninggatan 76 | 80 strandvägen | 81 malmskillnadsgatan | 82 hammargatan 2 | 83 rädmansgatan 39a | 84 hessensteinska huset | 85 stadshuset

VILNIUS

01 trakų gatvė 1 | 02 pylimo gatvė (sinagoga) | 03 arkikatedra bazilika | 04 aušros vartų | 05 didžioj gatvė 11 | 06 aušros vartų 13 | 07 gyneju gatvė 24 (nacionalinė biblioteka) | 08 didžioji tave | 09 stiklių gatvė 6 | 10 gedimino prospektas 51 | 11 pylimo gatvė 26 | 12 pilies gatvė 26 | 13 gedimino prospektas 53 | 14 gedimino prospektas/ gyneju gatvė 24 | 15 aušros tor | 16 žygimantų gatvė 10 |

17 stiklių gatvė 6 | 18 jono basanavičiaus gatvė 24 | 19 aušros vartų 4 | 20 katedros 1 | 21 jono basanavičiaus 8 | 22 didžioji gatvė 31 (rotušė) | 23 žygimantų gatvė 9 | 24 putino gatvė | 25 didžioji gatvė 34 | 26 pylimo gatvė 43 | 27 pilies gatvė 17 | 28 jono basanavičiaus gatvė 16 | 29 gedimino prospektas 53 (seismas) | 30 didžioji gatvė 31 | 31 pylimo gatvė 43 | 32 žygimantų gatvė 1 | 33 aušros vartų 6 (hotel europa royal) | 34 gedimino prospektas 51 | 35 pilies gatvė 6 | 36 dominikonu gatvė 2 | 37 aušros vartų 5 | 38 aušros vartų | 39 trakų gatvė 1 | 40 didžioji gatvė 34 | 41 jono basanavičiaus gatvė 4a | 42 totorių gatvė 29 | 43 bokšto gatvė 29 | 44 rūdninkų gatvė 118 | 45 didžioji gatvė 35/2 | 46 pilies gatvė 34 | 47 didžioji gatvė | 48 daukanto gatvė 3 | 49 1. stuokos-gucevičiaus gatvė 3 | 50 katedros 1 | 51 bokšto gatvė 19/12 | 52 rūdninkų gatvė 8 | 53 gedimino prospektas / gyneju gatvė 24 | 54 daukanto gatvė 3 | 55 aušros vartų 6 | 56 didžioji gatvė 4 | 57 didžioji gatvė 3 | 58 jono basanavičiaus gatvė | 59 daukanto gatvė 3 | 60 aušros vartų 6 | 61 trakų gatvė 1 | 62 j. tump-vaižganto 8a/ lukiškių 2 | 63 daukanto gatvė 1 | 64 voikečių gatvė | 65 didžioji gatvė 1 | 66 didžioji gatvė 34 | 67 žygimantų gatvė 9 | 68 universiteto gatvė 3/5

WIEN

01 fleischmarkt 13 | 02 hertha-firnberg-straße 7 | 03 guglgasse 43 | 04 marxergasse 32 | 05 carl-appelstraße 7 | 06 stammgasse 12 | 07 fleischmarkt 1 | 08 augustinerstraße 1 | 09 schmerlingplatz 6 | 10 stephansplatz 12 | 11 löwen-/ kegelgasse | 12 dr. karl renner ring 3 | 13 weiskirchstraße 3 | 14 guglgasse 13 | 15 aristide-de-sousa-mendes promenade | 16 carl-appelstraße 5 | 17 donau-city-straße 9b | 18 tegetthoffstraße 3 | 19 towerstraße (flughafen-tower) | 20 josefplatz | 21 nh-hotel airport | 22 museumsplatz | 23 wagramer straße 4a | 24 donau-city-straße 1 | 25 hertha-firnberg-straße 9 | 26 mariahilfer straße 32–34 | 27 opernring 2 | 28 carl-appelstraße 7 | 29 freyung 8 (kunstforum) | 30 herrengasse 11 | 31 wienerbergstraße 7 | 32 steyrerhof | 33 kegelergasse / lö-wengasse | 34 paragonstraße 1 | 35 wienerbergstraße 7 | 36 wagramer straße 4h | 37 vordere zollamtstorstraße 13 | 38 wagramer straße 4 | 39 kohlmarkt 8 | 40 wagramer straße 3–5 (uno city) | 41 franz josef kai 21 | 42 hertha-firnberg-straße 10 | 43 donau-city-straße 9e | 44 marxergasse 1b | 45 aristide-de-sousa-mendes promenade | 46 aristide-de-sousa-mendes promenade | 47 graben 23 | 48 guglgasse 13 | 49 paragonstraße 1 | 50 museumsplatz 1 | 51 carl-appelstraße 5 | 52 carl-appelstraße 7 | 53 augustinerstraße 1 | 54 uraniastraße 1 | 55 aristide-de-sousa-mendes promenade | 56 marc-aurel-straße 4 | 57 hertha-firnberg-straße 10 | 58 prater | 59 hertha-firnberg-straße 9 | 60 stephansplatz 12 | 61 donau-city-straße 1 | 62 marxergasse 1a | 63 donau-city-straße 9 | 64 donau-city-straße 1 | 65 stephansplatz 12 | 66 lugeck 2 | 67 plankengasse 4 | 68 marxergasse 1 | 69 augustiner straße 1 | 70 carl-appelstraße 7e | 71 museumsplatz 1 | 72 taborstraße 1–3 | 73 wagramer straße 8 | 74 hertha-firnberg-straße

ZÜRICH

01 plattenstrasse 14–20 | 02 poststrasse 12 | 03 hardturmstrasse 11 | 04 bahnhofstrasse 64 | 05 limmatquai 29 | 06 airport zürich-kloten | 07 am münsterhofplatz | 08 bahnhof stadelhofen | 09 karl-schmid-strasse 50–60 | 10 paradeplatz 8 | 11 airport zürich-kloten | 12 universität zürich zentrum (uzz) | 13 forchstrasse | 14 rämistrasse | 15 rämistrasse 71 | 16 münstergasse 3 | 17 augustinergasse 24 | 18 bahnhofstrasse 64 | 19 bahnhofstrasse 25 | 20 zürich-flughafen | 21 plattenstrasse 52 | 22 talstrasse 1 | 23 heimplatz 1 | 24 airport zürich-kloten | 25 bahnhof stadelhofen | 26 oranja strasse 6 | 27 am münsterhofplatz | 28 schipfe 2 | 29 schiffbaustrasse 4 | 30 zellweg 93 | 31 airport zürich-kloten | 32 falkenstrasse 1 | 33 seefeld | 34 forchstrasse 226 | 35 limmat-quai 29 | 36 schiffbaustrasse 11 | 37 airport zürich-kloten | 38 schiffbaustrasse 11 | 39 uraniastrasse 2a | 40 tannenstrasse 3 | 41 münsterhof 8 | 42 tannenstrasse 8 | 43 plattenstrasse 14/20 | 44 airport zürich-kloten | 45 limmatquai 19 | 46 hardturmstrasse 11 | 47 münstergasse 3 | 48 schiffbaustrasse 4 | 49 bahnhof stadlhofen | 50 schiffbaustrasse 18 | 51 talstrasse 1 | 52 schiffbaustrasse 4 | 53 bahnhofstrasse | 54 airport zürich-kloten | 55 zwinglihaus | 56 schiffbaustrasse 14 | 57 schiffbaustrasse 11 | 58 rämistrasse | 59 zürich-flughafen | 60 paradeplatz 8 | 61 bahnhofstrasse 63 | 62 zwingliplatz (großmünster) | 63 bahnhofstrasse 42 | 64 heinerplatz 1 | 65 rämistrasse 71 (uzz) | 66 hardturmstrasse 11 | 67 plattenstrasse 14/20 | 68 schiffbaustrasse 4 | 69 selnaustrasse 16–18 | 70 heimplatz 1 | 71 zollikerstrasse 130 | 72 tannenstrasse 9 | 73 rämistrasse 71 (uzz) | 74 universität zürich zentrum | 75 oberdorf | 76 schiffbaustrasse 4 | 77 talstrasse 1 | 78 airport zürich-kloten | 79 uraniastrasse 2a | 80 tannenstrasse 9 | 81 paradeplatz 6 | 82 paradeplatz 8 | 83 seefeld | 84 niederdorf | 85 bleicherweg | 86 niederdorf | 87 niederdorf | 88 villa in seefeld